Look Stunning At Any Size

An Everyday Woman's Guide to Looking Stylish

Parimita Chakravorty

V&S PUBLISHERS

Published by:

V&S PUBLISHERS

F-2/16, Ansari road, Daryaganj, New Delhi-110002
☎ 23240026, 23240027 • *Fax:* 011-23240028
info@vspublishers.com • www.vspublishers.com

Online Brandstore: amazon.in/vspublishers

Regional Office : Hyderabad
5-1-707/1, Brij Bhawan (Beside Central Bank of India Lane) Bank Street, Koti, Hyderabad - 500 095
☎ 040-24737290
vspublishershyd@gmail.com

Follow us on:

BUY OUR BOOKS FROM: AMAZON FLIPKART

ISBN 978-93-815884-8-2
New Edition

Introduction

This book is meant for all those women who think that looking good is a humongous and daunting task. Believe me, as long as you know what looks good on you, it's not. From 16 to 60, presenting oneself well is a common concern for us women. Looking good is a matter of confidence and social image.

I have come across several beautiful women, who at some point in their life took a beating on their self-confidence because of the way they looked during a particular phase in their life. Many medical conditions create physical changes which may be temporary, but leave a permanent impression on a woman's psyche. Women affected by cancer, thyroid or other hormonal imbalances, endometriosis, polycystic ovarian syndrome (PCOS), etc., have to cope with weight issues and other cosmetic let downs like blemishes, acne, facial hair, and various other symptoms. This book is dedicated to all those brave women who deal with such problems with a big smile. The book has information that will give them an insight into how to carry themselves well despite their temporary or permanent setbacks. This book also encourages them to be body confident and have a sense of style.

Along with suggesting everyone to cultivate their own style, I also believe that dressing with style is every woman's right. Feeling good about oneself is one of the basic pleasures any woman should, and must have. Every woman of any age wants to feel special.

You don't need to spend a fortune in doing so. With a bit of creativity, your wardrobe can be moulded into a style machine, bringing out the best in you.

This book is also dedicated to all those ladies who look into the mirror with displeasure and think that looking good is not their cup of tea. It's time they analysed themselves and understood what's stopping them from reinventing themselves.

Acknowledgements

I would like to thank all the eminent experts who added their domain insight in making this book useful and informative.

Special thanks to Ms Manishi Jain from Art of Make-up, Ms Shirin Merchant from Kut & Make Salon, Dr Rohini Wadhwani, Dr Preeti Savardekar, Dr Meha Mhatre, and Mr Pankaj Bhupatkar for guiding me on points that pertain to medicine, science, beauty, and technical know-how. Without their knowledgeable inputs it would have been unfair to comment on any treatment, styles, or products.

Heartfelt thanks to my dear husband for supporting and encouraging me throughout the journey of writing this book. Without his positivity and patience this book would have never seen the light of day. A big hug to both my sisters and mother who have always believed in me.

And last but not the least, a big thank you to my publisher who showed confidence in my work and encouraged me to finish this book. He patiently guided me in every step till the book took its final shape.

Prologue

25+, juggling career and romance, looking for a stable relationship to settle down after a few years. Have a steady boyfriend but unsure if he will walk down the aisle with you. And one fine morning he declares, "Look at X, Y, Z... They maintain themselves well. Perfect washboard abs!" You question yourself, "Does he mean I am fat? Does he not find me attractive?" And you hit the frenzy of severe exercising, numerous diets and pills, to get those washboard abs like X, Y, Z. You hate going out shopping with him because you feel embarrassed when the most 'in-style' jeans can't seem to fit your bottom. You look for the tallest heels to look a few more inches taller.

30+, overweight with a jelly-belly, frumpled look, not sure whether to attend to the crying baby or the lock of hair pricking your eyes. Walking with your husband in a mall or a multiplex, who is all praises for you but you perceive him to be a big 'Liar'. Then suddenly a young, slim and beautiful woman passes by and you can't help but notice that your husband is noticing her. You curse her under your breath, but your husband on the other hand turns around and says, "Darling! That was pretty loud." Yes! It does happen with quite a few. Most of us have lost the self confidence or rather the body confidence which was once a part of our personality.

We can't imagine someone appreciating us genuinely as we ourselves have a negative body image.

We seethe under our breath as we feel threatened by another pretty looking chic. Believe it or not, most women suffer from high insecurities and negative self-esteem.

Responsibilities of a married life and physical changes after pregnancy render many women incapable of taking care as they did before, much less appreciating themselves anymore; especially their bodies. Not only are these group of women affected by low self-esteem and hatred towards their own bodies, but they live in the false hope of returning to their youthful looks by adopting various fad diets and pills.

In the recent times a new breed of highly conscious women has grown by leaps and bounds (irrespective of their marital status). These are women who live in continuous denial. They do not want to accept the changes that time has bestowed upon them. Thanks to the size zero fad, and the 'Slim-is-in revolution,' most of them just don't have a healthy image about themselves. They try to emulate the rich and famous in their lifestyle and fashion sense without realising the outcome. What they also do not realise is that these celebrities put in hours of exercise and precise diet plans on a daily basis (which is difficult, though I won't say impossible) in our day-to-day life to look young and toned.

This book is not meant to discourage anybody from adopting a healthy lifestyle; instead it's aimed at appreciating and enhancing your current body type. Exercising and diet control are important changes an individual can apply to become fit (if not slim). But that's not what this book is all about. This book is a guide on how to present your current body with the correct fabric, cut, and style, and look stylish on all occasions. Learn to apply make-up in a manner that makes you look 'fab' instead of drab. You will also understand the correct way to use make-up for hiding your flaws and focus on your assets.

This, in short, is a style guide to help you make your own shopping list and guide you where to invest, what to wear and where.

This will also tell you what style essentials are and how to use them for your benefit. You will certainly grab all the attention that you desired, with new found confidence, poise, and enhanced looks.

Love yourself and respect your body! Take care of it as its vitality is precious.

Be fashion forward and fashion conscious but don't be a slave to fashion. Dress elegantly and you are bound to look great.

Love!

Contents

Chapter One

Know thyself

The first step to looking good is to appraise self

Have you ever asked yourself as to why you can't dress up as elegantly as the celebrities? Being body beautiful is one aspect of looking good, but what else adds to their charm? Perhaps their sense of style and the way they carry themselves. Just being body beautiful is not good enough. You need a unique sense of style to make a mark. And if you believe that looking good is just the prerogative of the rich and famous, then you are definitely wrong. You need not wear something expensive to look good, you should wear something good which looks expensive.

Style is personal; it is a form of self-expression.

But how many of us are interested in developing this aspect of our personality? Lack of motivation and creativity has led many women to believe that looking good is a luxury and not a necessity. Being comfortable in your own skin and presenting the best in you, gains more ground. Accept yourself the way you are and always try to be presentable. Dressing right is equally important.

What do I buy? What will look good on me?

Many women use their busy lives as the perfect foil to be short on time to look presentable. They also love to blame their own lack of attitude and resistance in cultivating a sense of style in their kids, husband, in-laws, work, office, neighbour, pet, and anyone they could get their eyes on.

They refuse to take out time for themselves. They feel guilty if they invest any time or money on their looks. What they don't realise however, is that this investment of time and money on their appearance will go a long way in boosting their self-confidence. Also, by doing so, they are not doing a favour to anybody. It is a necessary part of human psyche to look and feel good. They need to understand that they are doing this for themselves.

There are women who are dressed younger than their age; trying to give a stiff competition perhaps to their young nieces and daughters. Dress according to your age. A woman of any age can look absolutely stylish if she keeps in mind that she can't dress up like a teen queen all through her life.

And then there are a few who are young but dress like an old frumpy woman. They want to hide behind large clothes. Why hide behind your clothes? Make your clothes an ally rather than cocoon yourself in them.

The first step to looking good is to appraise oneself. Understanding your flaws and assets is a crucial part of looking your best.

Do you know yourself? No! This question isn't aimed at soul searching but more on how much do you know about yourself and your body? What shape is your body? What is your built? Or what bone structure do you have? What colour family will suit your complexion? What's your skin tone? What is the shape of your face? What hairstyles would suit your face shape? A bit of brainstorming and we all are ready to acknowledge the fact that we never pay attention to such details while shopping for clothes or choosing make-up. To top it all, most of us are not even aware about ourselves.

Know your body type

A body type can be recognised with the help of its bone structure and shape.

Let us understand the very basics of bone structure or body build:

Whenever you go shopping, you check the size of the apparel that you would want to buy. Generally, sizes vary from XS (extra-small), S (small), M (Medium) to

L (Large). The sizes beyond this like XL, XXL, XXXL, and above are termed in the category of plus size. Sizes are different for various brands so consider this as a general scenario.

Choose the correct size while shopping. Do not buy something which is smaller or larger than your size. Something which doesn't fit properly will be a waste as you will not like to wear that garment often or perhaps never. Don't get lured by the ideas that you can fit into the dress after two weeks of severe dieting. It doesn't work.

How can you judge what is your built or bone structure? You can easily find this out with the help of a thumb and forefinger test.

Let us assess your bone structure

Grasp your left wrist between your right thumb and right forefinger.

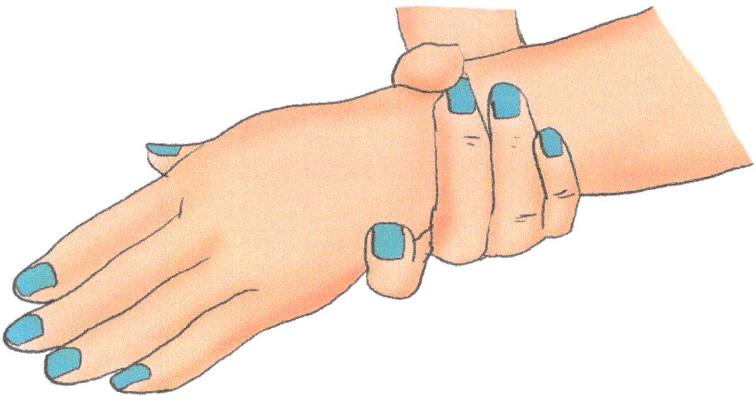

If you have a thin bone structure, the ends of your fingers overlap.

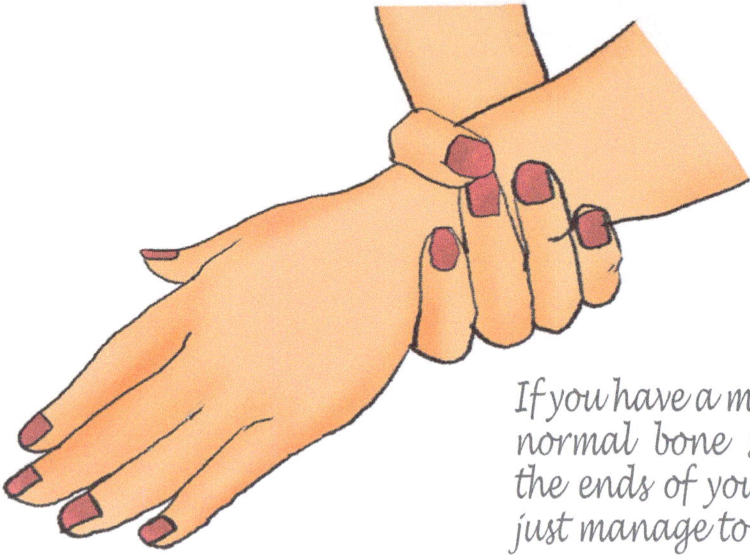

If you have a medium or normal bone structure, the ends of your fingers just manage to touch.

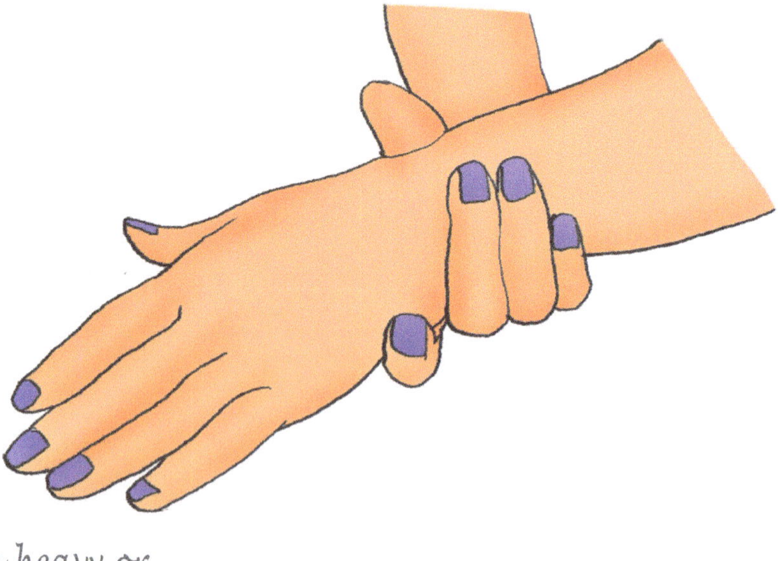

If you have a heavy or large bone structure, there is a gap between the ends of your fingers.

Once you are aware of your body built, you become far more realistic in terms of weight and your overall look as well as the final outcome after dressing up.

A 60 kg heavy-built woman can look slimmer than a 57 kg thin-bone structured woman. Every individual is unique in their own way. So stop comparing with others and focus on what assets you already have.

Once you know what your bone structure is like, then the next step is to ascertain your body type. It sounds foolish to cast one person into a particular body type. Every individual is different and can reflect a unique body shape. But to chalk out a graphic overview for easy understanding, let's get to the basics. Female body types are divided into six main categories; each one with a far more interesting name than the other. These are: the hourglass, the brick, the lollipop, the pencil, the apple, and the pear.

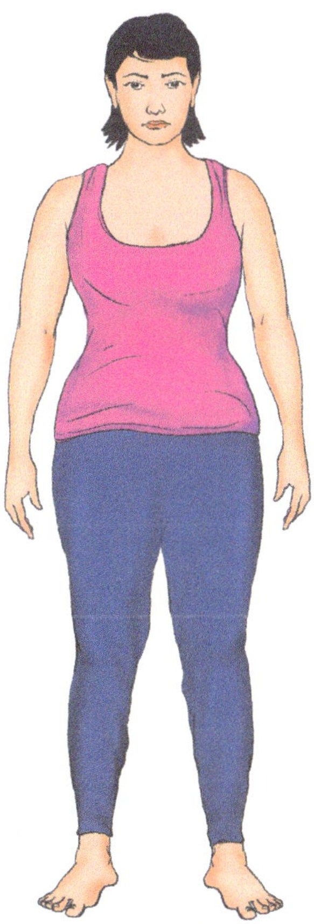

Hourglass

Hourglass shape: The hourglass shape is the most coveted shape of all times. Women with this shape are known for their curvaceous or voluptuous figure. Many women dream of acquiring this shape to look gorgeous. A natural hourglass figure may consist of any built. (Small, Medium, or Heavy, it doesn't matter and the same applies to other shapes as well). An hourglass shape would constitute big breasts, narrow waist, big hips, and generous thighs. They have gently rounded shoulders that align nicely with the hips. Hourglass shape has the ideal distribution of fat. For example a woman with 40-inch breast, 33-inch waist, and 41-inch hips can easily be termed an hourglass shape. (These statistics are based on real-life volunteers.) They have a "waist-to-hip ratio" of 0.7, or a waist measuring 70 per cent of the hip circumference.

Brick shape: A brick shape is usually a woman with a good built. Somebody who is athletic or a bit muscular can be easily termed as a brick shape. Alternatively, those who aren't muscular too can also fall into this category. Anybody with broad shoulders, non-existent waist, a flat bottom, chunky thighs and calves is considered to be a brick shape. A brick-shaped woman doesn't have many curves as her weight is evenly distributed throughout the body.

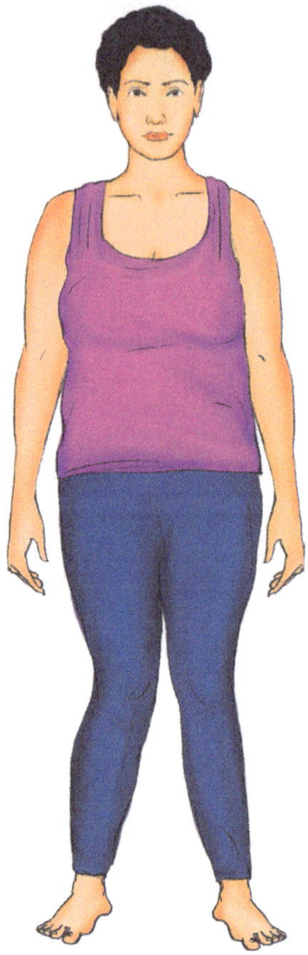

Brick

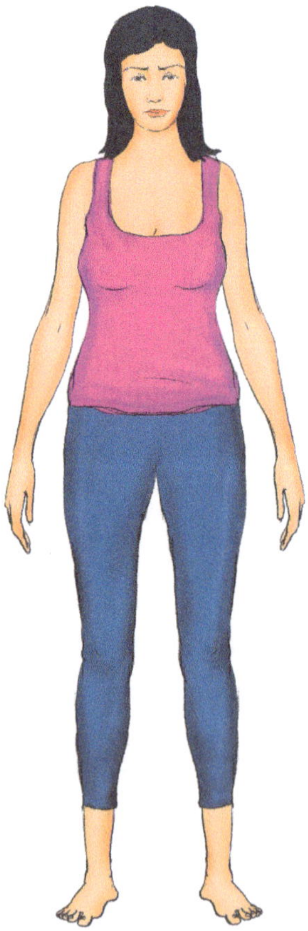

Lollipop

Lollipop shape: A lollipop-shaped woman will usually have big breasts, a slim waist, slim hips, and long legs. Women with this body shape are known for their Barbie doll figure. They are top heavy; narrowing all the way down. They have slender shoulders which are not proportionate to their hips. Lollipop shapes are a rage among the youth these days as everyone wants to look slim with bigger breasts. A few celebrities even go under the knife to get this shape.

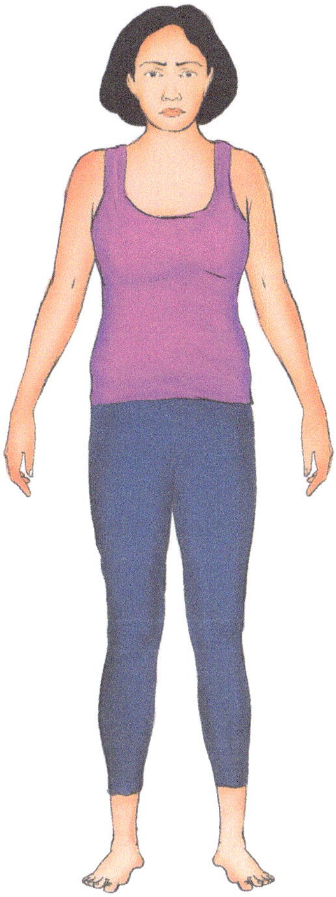

Pencil

Pencil shape: A pencil shape is the one in which a woman looks pencil straight or uniformly lean. From top to bottom, she has a slim silhouette or boyish structure, and doesn't have many curves either. They look taller than they actually are. Most ramp models fall in this category. Though their stick thin structure is ideal in the fashion circle but in real life, it might be difficult to dress them up. The main idea is to create womanly curves on their body shape.

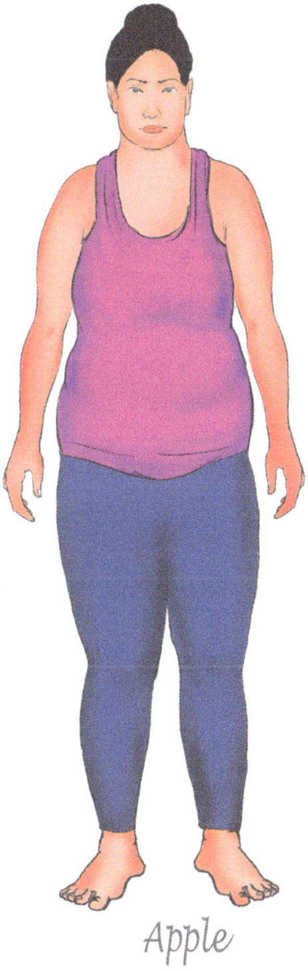

Apple

Apple shape: An apple shape is anybody with an average breasts, heavier around the middle with flat bottom and average legs. The focus is on the mid-section as it is the widest. Their breast and middle look out of proportion though their limbs look slim and proportionate. They usually have a wide back and shoulders which can be used to ones advantage while dressing. It is a very common shape; and is the most difficult to dress.

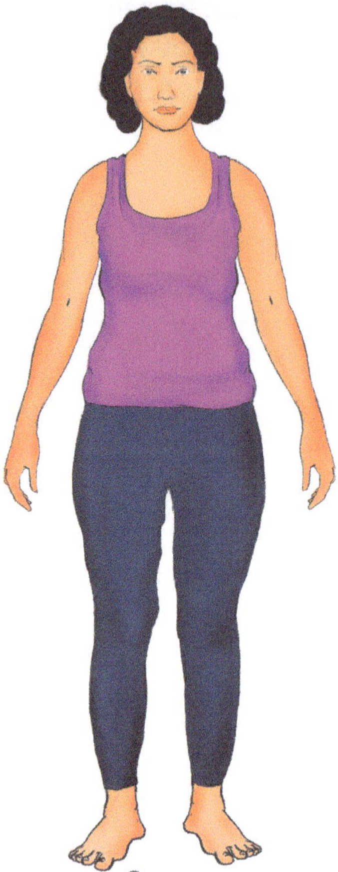

Pear

Pear shape: A pear-shaped woman has small breasts, long waist, big hips, saddle bags, and heavy thighs and buttocks. A pear is characterised by extra weight on the outer thighs. A pear-shaped woman may have chunky calves. They are curvaceous around the hip but smaller at the top. The focus is largely around the bottom. They might appear a bit heavy than they really are, but they have a slim neck, shapely breasts, slender shoulders, and a defined waist. They might also have shapely limbs. While dressing they should try to highlight these body parts.

Once you are sure about your body type, you can look closely at your face. Do you know what is the shape of your face? It's really important to know your face shape as then you can get the right haircut and apply the correct make-up to accentuate your overall look.

Know your face shape

Your face is the window to the world, your source of expression, depicting your beauty and character. To highlight its beauty, you'll need to know what looks good on it. The same is the case with hairstyle and make-up. Both these, if known correctly, can accentuate your facial features, making you look more attractive.

Let's assess your face structure

Just like body shape, it is very difficult to assess one's face shape. Every individual has been gifted with certain characteristics that are unique. Experts have listed 6 basic face cuts that can help us get a general overview about the face structure. These are: Oval, Round, Rectangle or Oblong, Square, Heart, and Triangle face shape.

So how does one determine the shape of your face?

It's easy really if you have a handy measuring tape.

To find out the shape of your face, first tie your hair tight into a ponytail. Make sure there are no flyaways, and then measure it with a measuring tape.

Take the following measurements and write down the measurement on a piece of paper:

1. Measure your face across the top of your cheekbones.
2. Measure across your jaw line from one widest point to the other.
3. Measure across your forehead at the widest point.
4. Measure from the tip of your hairline to the bottom of your chin.

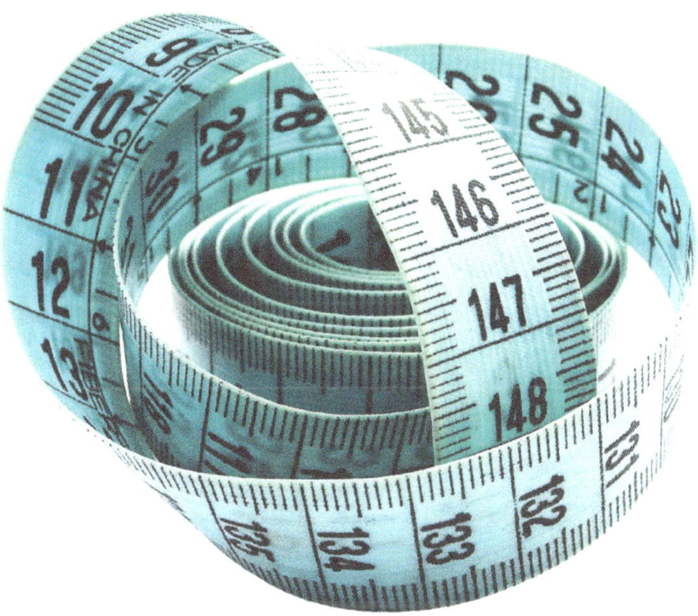

Measuring tape

Now measure all the dimensions to find out your face shape:

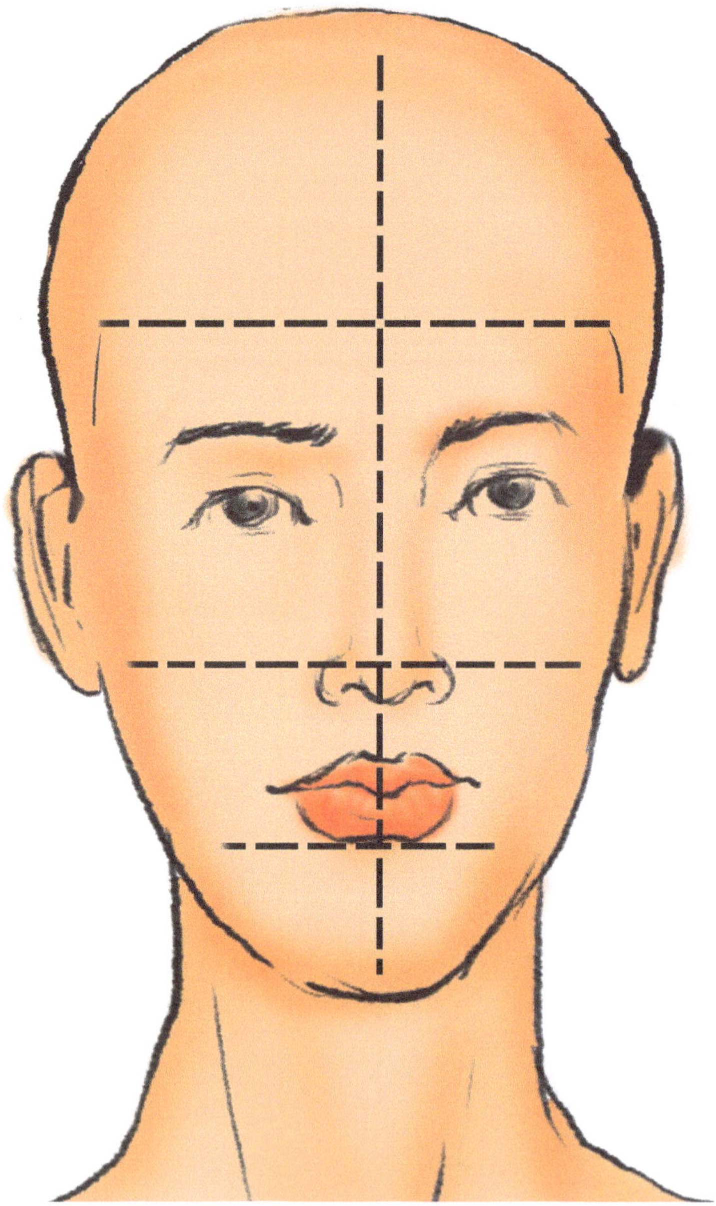

Face shape

Oval face shape: This is considered to be the perfect face shape and is the easiest to style. An oval face shape will have wider cheekbones and then narrow down to the jaw line and chin. Oval face shape will also be narrow up towards the forehead. If your measurement is widest along the cheekbones and your forehead and chin are proportionately same, then you have an oval face.

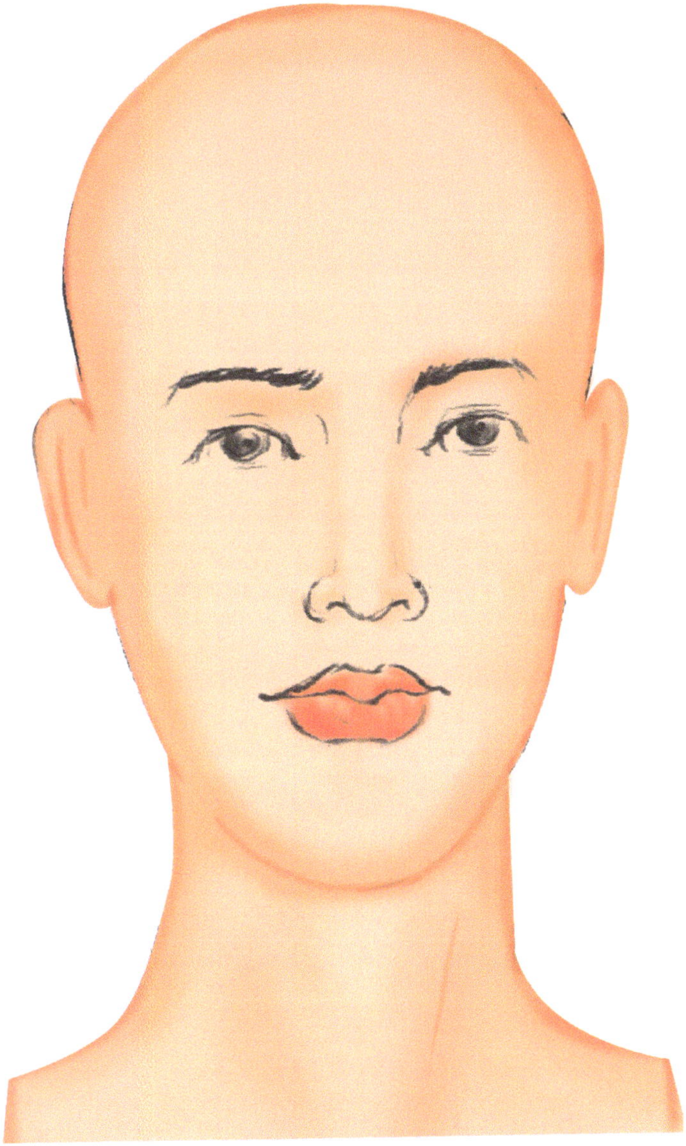

Oval face

Heart face shape: A heart-shaped face is very unique. It will be broader at the forehead and then taper into a small, narrow chin. If the measurements suggest that your face is widest at the forehead and slimmer around chin and jaw line, then you have a heart-shaped face. A heart-shaped face usually looks attractive due to its distinct shape.

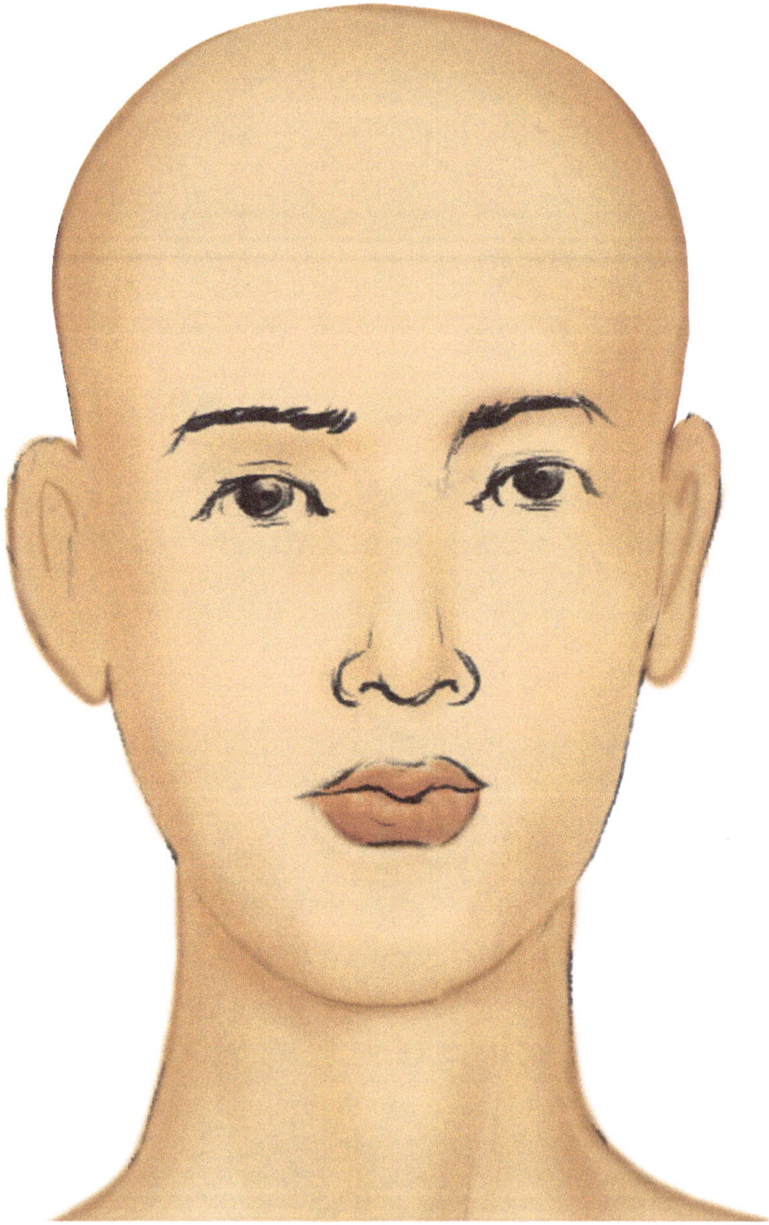

Heart face

Triangle face shape: A triangle face will be wider at the cheeks and jaw but have a narrow forehead. If the measurements suggest that your face is widest at the jaw line but narrow along the forehead, then you have a triangle-shaped face.

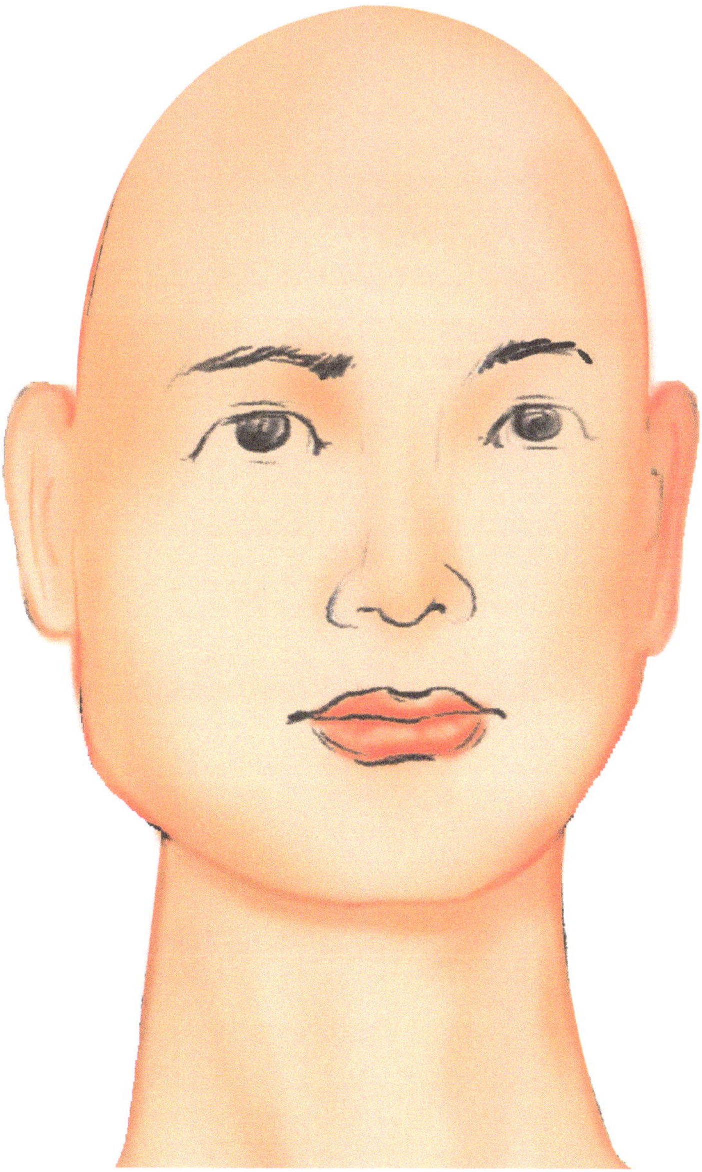

Triangle face

Square face shape: A square face is very common. It will be equally wide at the forehead, cheeks, and jaw line. If the measurements suggest that your face proportionately measures the same throughout jaw line, forehead and the length between hairline and chin, then you can easily conclude that you have a square-shaped face.

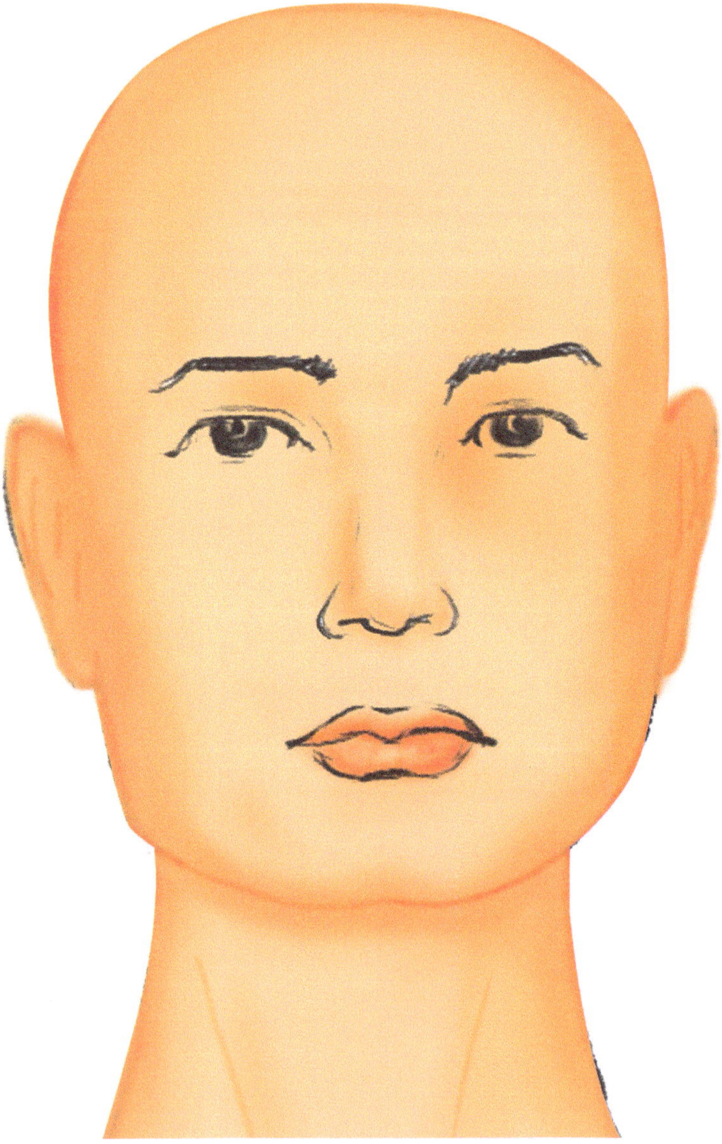

Square face

Round face shape: Round face shapes are fuller and will usually look younger than they are. It will have a round forehead and a round chin, with wide, full cheeks. If your measurements suggest that your hairline to chin is equal to the measurement across your cheekbones, then you have a round face.

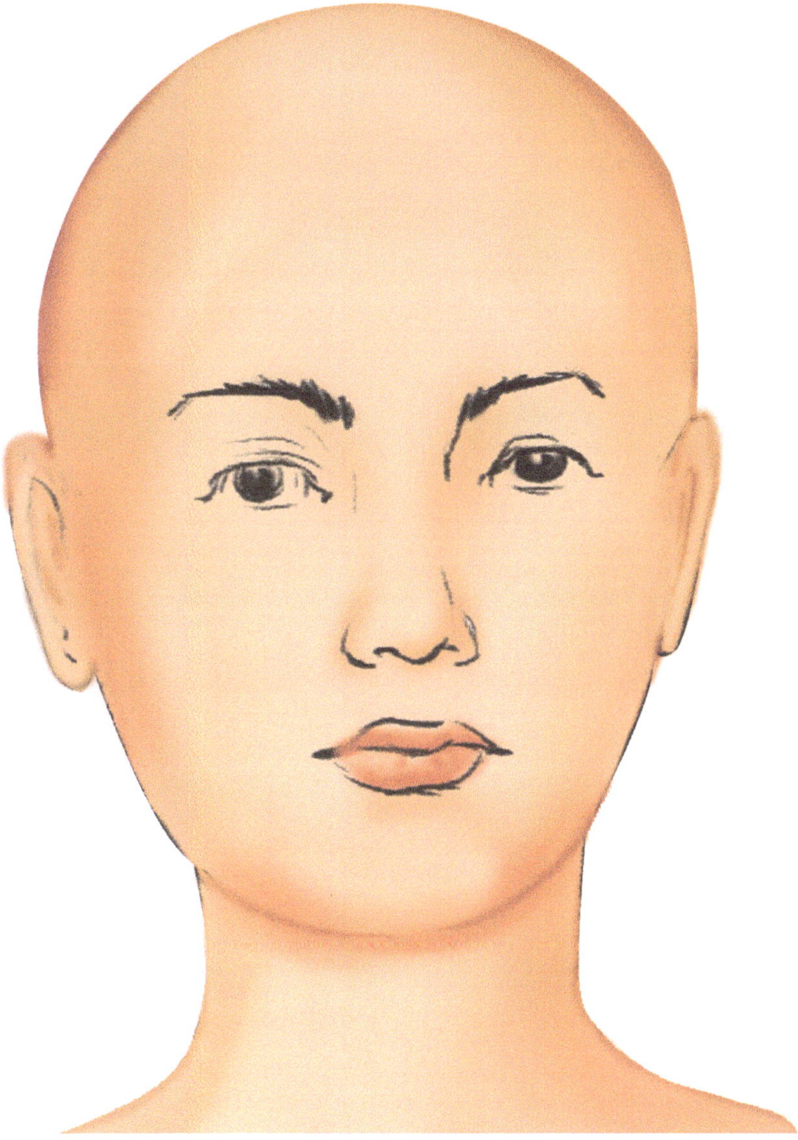

Round face

Rectangle face shape: A rectangle face shape is similar to an oval face shape but has broad cheekbones, a broad jaw line, and a broad forehead. If your measurement suggests that your face is longer from hairline to chin as compared to the length across the cheekbones, but your forehead measures the same as your jaw line, then you have a rectangle face cut.

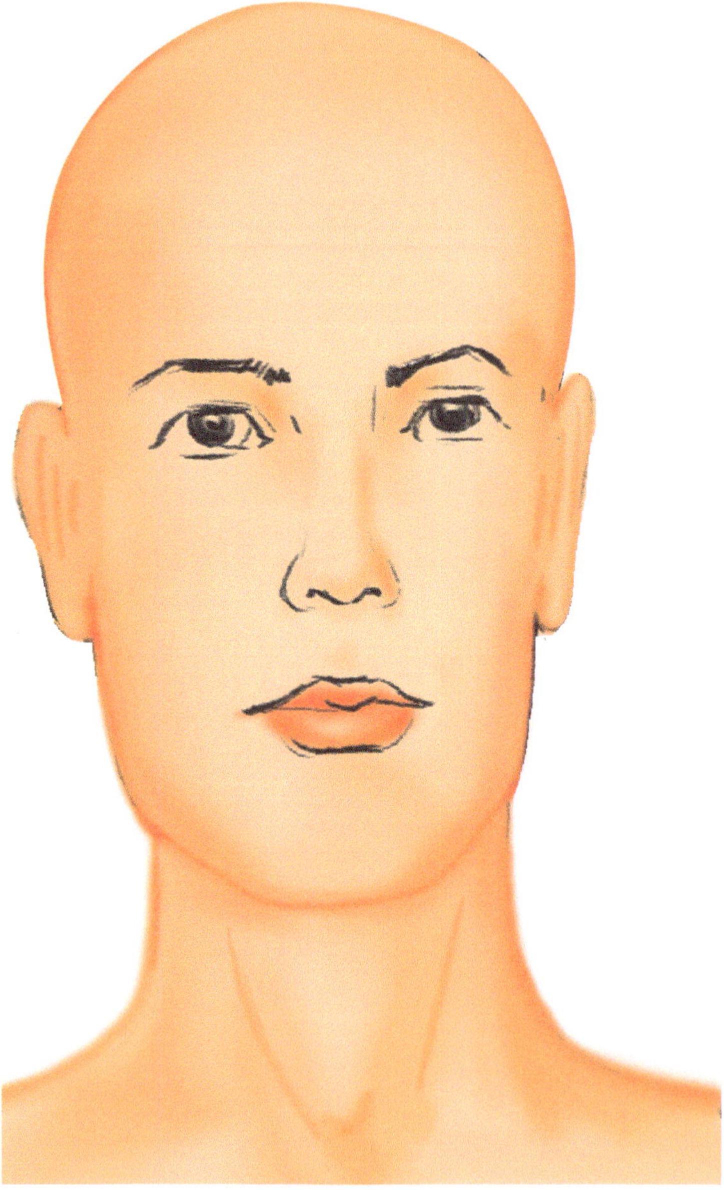

Rectangle face

Once you are sure about your face shape, it will be easy for you to decide what make-up to use and highlight which features (details given in the forthcoming chapters). You can also ascertain which hairstyle will make you look sassy and chic (these too are listed further on).

Know your skin tone

Knowing your skin tone is absolutely necessary while choosing the colour of your make-up, accessories, and apparel. The right colour can enhance your look and the wrong one can kill your entire ensemble. So be very sure about your skin tone. It is easy to know your skin tone.

Skin tones are categorised as cool, warm, or neutral.

1. **Cool skin tone:** If your skin looks good in blue, pink, fuchsia, and all shades in between, then you have a cool skin tone. Another great way of knowing your skin tone is through the colour of your veins reflected from beneath the skin. Also, if your veins look blue in colour then you have a cool skin tone. If you easily get sun burnt and you look pinkish in extreme cold or hot weather then also you have a cool skin tone.
2. **Warm skin tone:** If your skin looks good in orange, red, green, and all shades in between, then you have a warm skin tone. Also, if your veins look green in colour beneath your skin then you have a warm skin tone. If you easily get tanned in the sun and you look yellowish or greenish in extreme hot or cold weather then you have a warm skin tone.
3. **Neutral skin tone:** If your skin looks good in peach, yellow, or olive greens, and if you look pale in cold months, then you have a neutral skin tone. Neutral skin tones are those with no obvious overtones of yellow or pink. They look good in autumn shades. If you're not sure, a beauty advisor at a cosmetics counter can advise you correctly.

Once you know yourself, the journey ahead will be a lot simpler. You will know exactly what to choose while getting dressed. In the next section we will see how you can enhance your look by choosing the right dress based on your body type. This style guide is for both Indian as well as western wear and you may mix and match to create your own style now that you are aware of your bone structure, body shape, face shape, and skin tone.

The key here is to experiment. One look might work for a person but may not work for another. So, keep an open mind and don't forget to try out new things. Eventually, you will discover a style which will be unique to you.

You look great, and with perfect dressing and style you will look gorgeous.

Chapter Two

Dress according to your body type

Create a balanced body shape through dressing

Shopping for clothes is hard work or even a mammoth task if you are not sure what looks good on you. Getting bouts of depression on the very first trial where either your breasts or your bottoms don't fit in right is rather common, so relax! Use the hints to choose the right dress for you. Make your shopping experience more joyful and your wardrobe better by applying these tips.

Stay off the frustration if standard fits aren't right for you. A bit of creativity and imagination, and you can create your own masterpiece with some innovations. This section will highlight the body types and list a few guidelines while choosing the right attire for you.

The key here is to balance; create a balanced body shape through dressing.

Read the tips for all body types, so that you know what works for you and what works for others. Apply it to your dressing and you can look marvellous. Try and add some zing to your not so favourite body parts by wearing clothes which compliment your body shape and make your entire frame proportionate.

Quick Tip: Don't ever buy in bulk. If one T-shirt or kurti fits you, don't go ahead and buy all colours available in that range. Invest wisely in quality apparel, rather than spending on quantity. And don't forget our dear 'tailor'. A bit of alteration comes handy while trying to get a perfect fit and there is no harm in investing some money and time on the tailoring and fitting of a dress if it makes you look like a million bucks.

To be honest, a girl's wardrobe can never have enough dresses, shoes, or bags. The accessories, bags, and shoes are a must for experimenting different looks. But let's list a few essentials that go a long way in keeping the art of dressing alive and kicking. Yes! Everybody loves to dress but the basic essentials are sometimes forgotten. Let's find out the minimum necessities every woman should have in her wardrobe, for a great dressing experience.

The Essentials

Western wear

- A white front-button shirt. This can be teamed with a denim waistcoat for a casual look or a blazer for a formal look.
- A white T-shirt
- A black pant suit
- A soft neutral suit with pants or a skirt (grey, brown, khaki)
- Denim jacket
- 2 pairs of neutral trousers
- 2 cotton front button shirts
- 2 evening wear dresses
- 2 party tops
- 3 pairs of jeans (all hemmed to different lengths for flats, heels, and sandals)
- The Little Black Dress (LBD)
- A summer blazer
- A winter coat
- A pair of winter gloves (to keep yourself warm)
- A head warmer

Western wear

Indian wear

- ☞ A black saree with a border (always helps to dress formally for any occasion, but make sure it doesn't have too many embellishments)
- ☞ A Chiffon saree (to quickly get into the 6 yards without asking help from our mommy or granny)
- ☞ A formal Churidar kurta in neutral colours like off-white, apple white, beige, pinks, blues (not the baby pinks and blues please!) etc., (to appear for interviews or official visits)
- ☞ A bright floral Churidar kurta with flared hems and if possible, sleeveless (to go out with your in-laws or with your husband to a traditional yet casual occasion)
- ☞ 2 to 3 short kurtis which fit well and are nicely teamed up with your patiala salwars or skinny jeans

Indian wear

Innerwear

- ☞ Good fitting bras (this is the best investment for any woman)
- ☞ Control pants or shapers (husbands/ boyfriends usually call them tummy holders)
- ☞ A long camisole covering your thighs (helps to wear dresses with light fabric)
- ☞ Body suits (many hate the mention of these lung-wrenching innerwear but it helps to decrease a few inches in a jiffy)

Innerwear

Accessories

- 2 watches
  (one leather and one link band)
- 1 black bag
- 1 brown bag
- 1 colour or print bag
- Black heels
  (Heels could be platform or low)
- Brown heels
- White heels
- Embellished heels
- 2 flats
- Black boots
- Ear studs in diamante
- Earrings in silver
- Bracelets in black, brown, diamante
- Heavy neckpiece

Accessories

Make-up

- Mascara
- Smudge-proof liner
- Kajal
- Neutral pink lipstick
- A tinted moisturiser
- Concealer
- Baby wipes or facial wipes (It helps in removing make-up and dirt without damaging your skin)
- Sunscreen (it is a must, follow it like a religion, never skip)

Make-up

The list is endless but we are talking just about the essentials. So let's keep it simple!

Quick Tip: The next thing you would want to do is clean up your wardrobe and put all the pieces that you have not worn over a year into one big box. Don't think that you might fit into those dresses someday (that day usually never comes). A clean and organised wardrobe is the best way to decide what you want to wear and the clothes also remain in good shape. All sarees you wore around your wedding but do not intend to wear anymore, the dresses from your honeymoon that do not fit you anymore, and other itsy bitsy stuff you have accumulated over a period of time should go away. Throw away the shoes which do not fit, are not comfortable, damaged or are just lying unused on your shoe rack. The dust gathered on them is an evidence that they have not kissed your feet for long and might not be used in the future as well. Moreover, wearing wrong-sized and uncomfortable shoes may lead to medical complications for your feet which I am sure you don't want.

Just sit for a while and think what all have you stuffed in your wardrobe for the sake of emotional attachment. If the jacket bought by your first boyfriend doesn't fit, it needs to go. The traditional dress from Singapore (an impulsive purchase from your honeymoon) is lying useless as a memento, it's time for it to go as well.

Once you have put the unnecessary stuff into that box, let your creative juices flow. May be a saree can be tailored into an evening dress or a Churidaar kurta for formal occasions. A great skirt may be tailored into a well-fitting top. An embellished jacket might be converted into a clutch. Loose jeans may be tailored into great shorts. There are innumerable ways of creating something new and unique from your old stuff. So choose and keep aside what you feel you can transform in the near future. Make sure to take it to the tailor and discuss your ideas at the earliest. Ideas shouldn't stagnate in your mind and the same applies to your chosen clothes in the box.

Customised Tailoring

The rest of the stuff, including shoes, can be kept for your immediate family and friend's perusal. If they like something, they might pick it up for themselves. In this process your wardrobe becomes clean and more organised.

Now let us look at the pointers which will help you know what to wear according to your body type. Although this is just an overview and will help you to choose the dresses to look your best; always remember to wear something which fits you well and makes you feel comfortable. When you feel beautiful, you look beautiful. Always keep this in mind so that your dress makes you feel attractive, automatically reflecting this in your attitude.

Hourglass

Tops: If you are an hourglass lady, you should accentuate your feminine curves with V necks, fitted tops, T-shirts, and vests. Define your tops with slim belts. You can also emphasise your lean waist with oversized shirts which come with built-in belts. Summer blazers or denim jackets with a V neck, if teamed with a tee, will make you look irresistible.

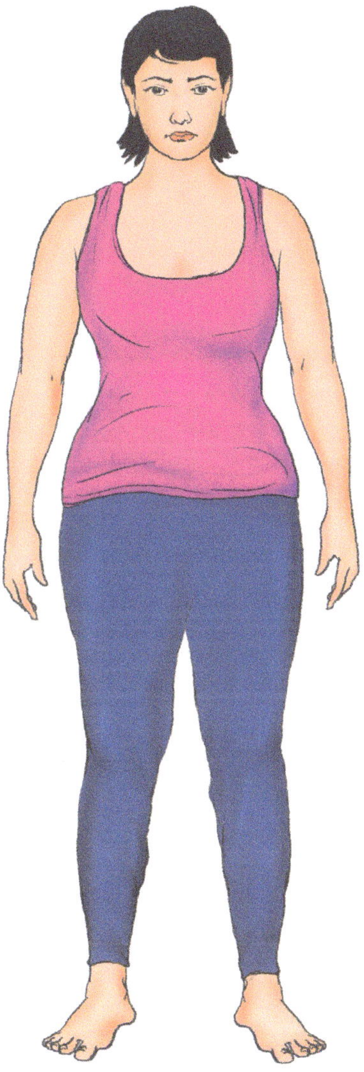

Hourglass

Bottoms: Wear flared skirts which clasp around the waist and highlight your slim waist. Add a belt and accentuate your curves. A pencil skirt will look equally flattering. Wear flat front trousers and avoid side pockets.

Dresses: Wear a waist-defining belted dress in bright colours or floral prints. Slimming vertical-striped dresses or monochromatic dresses will also look good on you. Your body shape is very feminine so any dress which is classy and has defined cuts will make you look like a lady.

Jeans: Straight leg jeans in dark colours will look great on you. You can also try boots.

Accessories: A bright clutch will draw attention to your waist. Avoid killer heels. Choose shoes with rounded or peep toes.

Beachwear: V-neck kaftans will flatter your bust. Tunics also look great. Go for a tie-neck bikini top and simple bikini bottom.

Sarees: Keep the prints sublime and smaller. A bold border would highlight your shape.

Kurtis: Short tunic kurtis with tights would look great on you. If your arms are heavy, make sure you wear three-quarter sleeves.

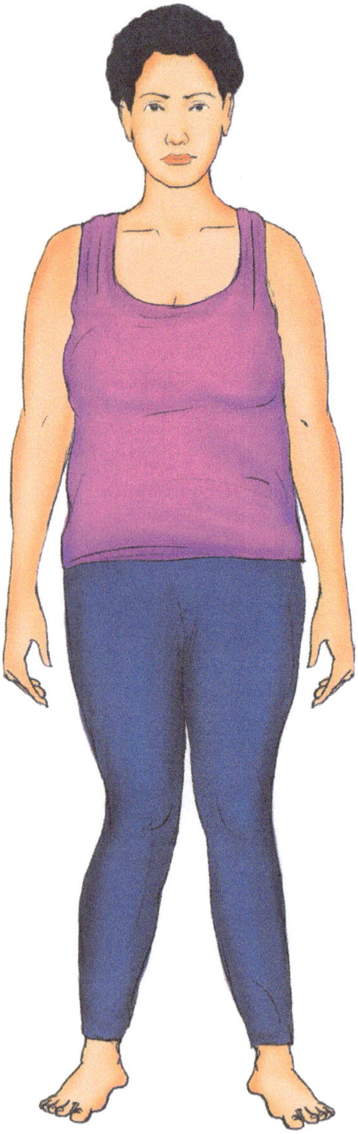

Brick

Brick

Tops: Bricks usually look boyish, so they should try to build feminine curves as much as possible with their dressing. Wear long length T-shirts and vests, define it with heavy belts to create an illusion of a slimmer waist. Oversized shirts with built-in belts will also give you the same effect. Jackets that are buttoned around the waist will give you curves. Long T-shirt dresses with a scowled neck will round you up at the top. Tops with sequins around the neck will add a feminine touch and roundness.

Bottoms: Tulip or long-flared skirts will help you create curves around your hip. Add a belt and create curves around the middle. A-line skirts with asymmetric pleats will look equally flattering on your shape.

Dresses: Slimming vertical-striped dresses or monochromatic dresses will look good on you. Dresses with bright prints or with layers and ruffles will create fullness to your shape.

Jeans: Straight leg jeans in dark colours will look great on you. You can also try boot-cut jeans with medium heels.

Accessories: Wedge heels and killer heels are the best way to lengthen your legs. Go for rounded toes to add some curves to your look.

Beachwear: Bright-coloured bikini sets and kaftans with a belt will look good on you.

Sarees: Bright and bold floral designs, stripes, and bigger prints will make you look feminine and curvaceous. Try to avoid borders. Avoid sarees in pure cotton as they fluff up and can make you look bulky. Try delicate fabrics instead.

Kurtis: A-line kurtis which end above your knee or slightly below your knee will suit you. Team up kurtis with tights and you would look curvaceous. Cap sleeves are best to show off your toned arms.

Lollipop

Tops: Try to wear bustiers with boyfriend blazers or jackets. They will shift the focus from your top and make them look smaller. Tops with high collars will also give the same effect. You can try square necks to give a geometric edge to your fuller bosoms.

Bottoms: The idea is to make your lower portion appear fuller. A pencil skirt with a slightly ruffled hem, harem pants, a fringed skirt with gladiator sandals will divert the attention from your upper body and create an illusion of a fuller bottom. Bell bottom trousers will balance your body shape so that you look less top heavy.

Dresses: Tulip dress will emphasise your hips and balance your body. Dresses with colour blocks and floral prints will look good on you as they add fullness to the body shape. Just make sure that they are simple at the top.

Jeans: Wide leg or straight cut are the ones for you. They will help to balance your body shape.

Accessorise: Big bold earrings will keep eyes at face level. Also, long but slim neckpieces will draw the attention towards your middle. You should wear killer heels or shoes with slim heels to put focus on your long, shapely legs.

Beachwear: One piece swimsuit with a deep V neck, kaftans for beachside cocktails, and dark-coloured bikinis will suit you the best.

Sarees: Bright, small floral designs, and smaller prints with borders will help to remove focus from your top. Try to wear sarees in pure fabrics like jute, cotton, etc., which will make you look fuller from the waist down.

Kurtis: Flared hem kurtis which end above your knee are best for you. Flared kurtis with tights have been sported by many stars and are best for the lollipop body shape. Go sleeveless if you have slender and toned arms.

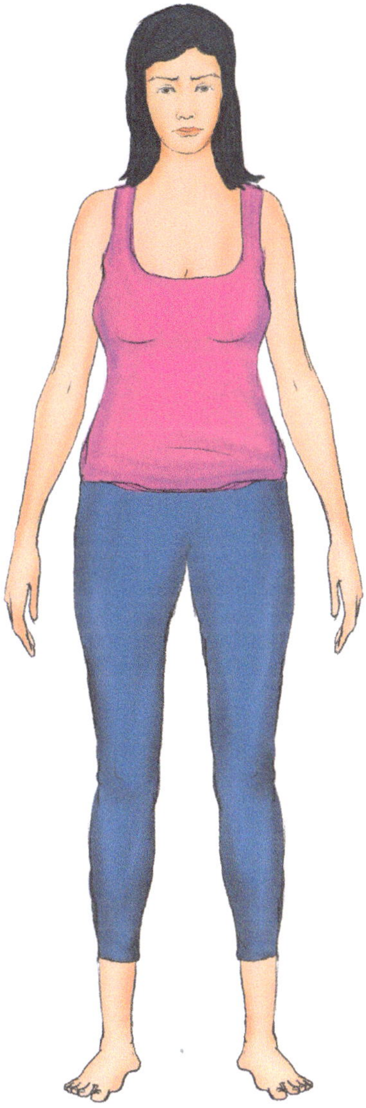

Lollipop

Pencil

Tops: Pencil body shapes are slender and delicate throughout. They feel the need to widen up the torso. Wide necklines and capped sleeves will help to broaden your shoulders. To add curves to your chest, wear tops with ruffles or pleats down the front. Gathering and pleating on the shirt will add a spherical shape to your overall look. Try tops that flaunt your back and shoulders.

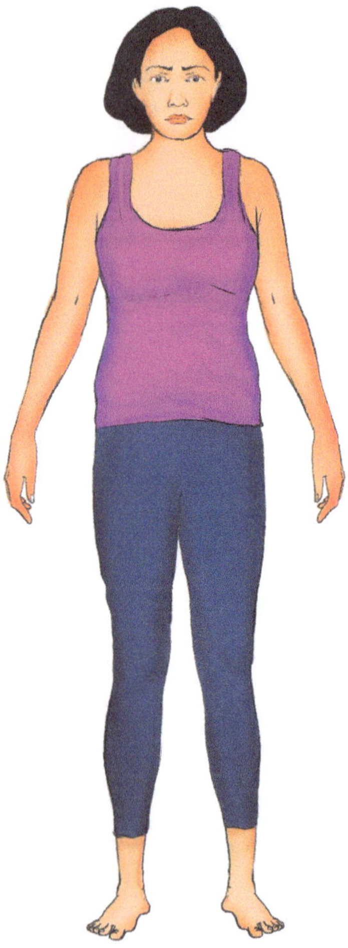

Pencil

Bottoms: Jumpsuits and playsuits will make you look curvaceous. Miniskirts, bright or patterned leggings, and voluminous harem pants will

Dresses: A dress with slight ruffles from waist till the thighs will add curves to your hips. Try to get embellished, printed, with a bow, or a ruffled dress as all these add volume to a shape. A feminine chiffon dress will soften your shape even while you add volume. The key is to look shapely and not bulky.

Jeans: Skinny jeans look great on you because you have a pair of long slender legs.

Accessories: Wear massive but supportive heels and chunky jewellery to add volume to your look. Oversized sunglasses and bright printed scarves are ideal for drawing attention to your face.

Beachwear: You can carry off any style with élan. You can mix and match top and bottom. Wear brightly-coloured kaftans and stretchy bandeau dresses to cover up in style.

Sarees: Wear sarees in pure fabrics like jute and cotton which make you look fuller from waist down. Sarees with embellishments and heavy borders will also make you look fuller.

Kurtis: Short A-line kurtis with embellishments around the neck will look good on you. The length should end a few inches above your knee and once you team them with patiala salwars, it will add to the zing. Go sleeveless if you have slender and toned arms and three-quarter sleeves if you have heavy arms.

Apple

Tops: Your tops should be loose fit and must have a long length. A tunic top flatters you. You can use buttoned-up summer blazers to get a slimmer look. Fringed waistcoats and jackets will help to draw the attention below the hips.

Bottoms: Go for jumpsuits that clinch you just below the bust line or bottoms with a lot of ruching and fabric around the waist. Tie waist belts to create an illusion of a slimmer waist. Flat front or high-waisted trousers will give you a smooth look. Try A-line skirts, fringed skirts, or trousers with side fastening.

Dresses: Wrap dresses look great on you as they highlight the slimmest part of your body which is usually just below your bra line. Get a LBD with draping or pleating for various occasions. A LBD with delicate jewellery is good for a formal evening and a LBD with a summer blazer or printed jacket is equally good for day-time wear or office wear. Try bright dresses with a waist band or a different-coloured belt to highlight the slimmest portion of your body.

Jeans: Go for wide bottom fits or boy fits. This will give you an effortless slim look and keep the attention on your legs. Wide bottom or flared jeans also elongate your legs.

Accessories: Statement necklaces, geometric mid-size bags, and large sunglasses draw attention upwards and make you look smaller around the middle. You can use a good printed scarf to draw attention towards your face. A small wedged heel or medium heels with pointed toes are suitable to highlight your shapely ankles.

Beachwear: Tankinis or one-piece suits are ideal for you. Look for V necks or asymmetric one shoulder suits to draw attention upwards.

Sarees: Fine prints, and small floral designs without borders will help to remove focus from your middle. Wear delicate fabrics like chiffon to have less volume around the middle.

Kurtis: A-line long kurtis which end below your knee are the best for you. Dark-coloured kurtis with light-coloured tights will look best on you and shift the focus to your legs from the middle. Full or three-quarter sleeves are best if your arms are heavy. Vertical stripes will make you look slimmer and taller.

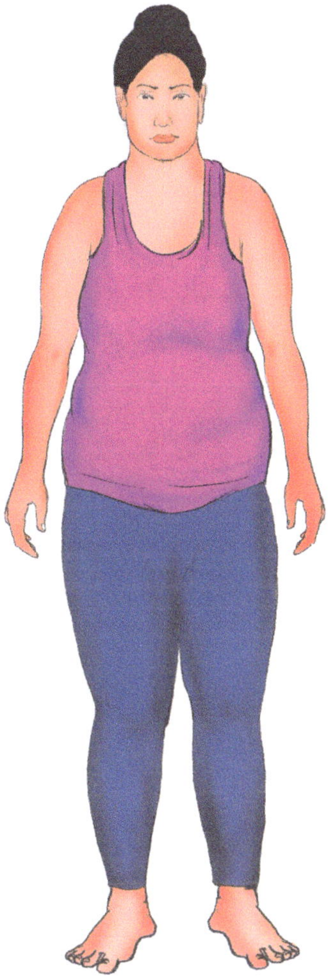

Apple

Pear

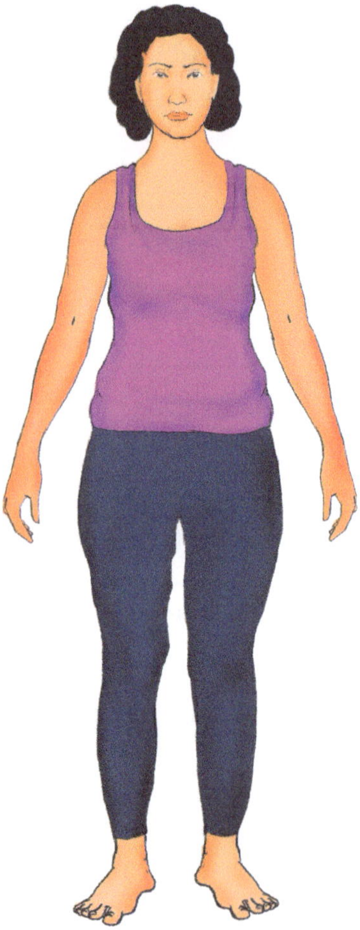

Pear

Tops: Drawing attention upwards is a great way of flattering your body shape. Floral, bright-coloured tops are a must. Delicate and strappy tops will also look good because of your humble breasts. Tops that widen your shoulders also balance your hips. Choose embellished, asymmetric, or slash necklines. Capped or frill sleeves are perfect for you.

Bottoms: Dark-coloured bottoms will make your hips look smaller. Avoid side pockets and go for flat front trousers. Wide leg trousers will balance your silhouette. A-line skirts will flare over your hips giving an illusion of a slim waist and balanced hips. Show off your legs in three-quarter pants.

Dresses: Shoulder and strapless dresses will help divert the focus to the upper part of the body. Wear long dresses to cover your heavy hips and thighs. Maxi dress will look good on you.

Jeans: Boot cut jeans and flared jeans will help to balance your hips. Super flared jeans are ideal if you wish to cover your thighs. Wear it with block and wedge heels to elongate your legs.

Accessorise: Printed scarves, chunky jewellery and big shoppers will help divert the attention upwards. Cone heels will look good on you.

Beachwear: Wear simple dark bikini bottoms with a bright top or halter neck to draw attention upwards. You can also try an asymmetric one-piece swimsuit.

Sarees: Fine prints in dark colours will make you look slim. Slim borders or no border will look good on you. Wear delicate fabrics which don't fluff up around your waist and hip area.

Kurtis: Short kurtis with a belt will help to balance your heavy hips. Short kurits also broaden your shoulders. Flared kurtis below the knee with tights are best for your body shape. Go sleeveless if you have slender and toned arms.

Winter wear

Northern India and a few states in the eastern part of our country get an extreme cold weather where you can sport your winter coats and parkas for a couple of months. Make sure you invest in the right pieces. Though for a few months, but you should cover yourself in style.

Forget your grandma-woven pullovers and cardigans for a while and get yourself stylish warm jumpers and coats according to your body type; team them up with the right accessories to look your best.

Wear a good waist belt on your jumpers, or a thin belt on the cardigans to accentuate your curves. Let us look at the few pointers on how to choose the right winter wear according to your body shape.

- If you are petite and fuller, try a cropped jacket to make you look taller. If you intend to wear a long overcoat, make sure it is dark coloured.
- If you are an hourglass figure, try a quilted parka and tie the belt around your waist, accentuating your shape. A trench coat is perfect for your shape.
- If you are the lollipop shape or have a fuller bust, wear a double-breasted coat or parka to make the bust line appear smaller. Military coat is also suitable for you.

Winter wear

- ☞ If you are pencil or boyish shape, wear leather bomber jackets with a dress to look young and curvaceous.
- ☞ If you are an apple or pear shape, wear A-line coats which are well fitted around your bust but loose around your waist and thighs.
- ☞ If you are brick shaped, get the feminine curves with the help of tulip parkas or flared hem coats.
- ☞ Get a good hat or cap, muffler, and gloves set to go with your coat.

Don't fear experimenting or mixing and matching. These tips will just help you highlight your assets and camouflage your faults. Nobody is perfect, so focus on the best and hide the rest. Once you are clear about dressing according to your body type, the next thing you would want is to choose the right colour as per your skin tone.

Chapter Three

Wear colours as per your skin tone

People who understand colour look more interesting, confident, self assured, and attractive as colours affect the way you look

Once you have sorted out the dress style and shape, then the next thing to keep in mind for looking your best is to wear the right coloured dresses and accessories. Colour plays a vital part in our lives. It appeals to our senses and attracts attention. The right colour can put a glow on your face and a wrong colour can just make you look pale and haggard.

Everybody's skin tone is divided into warm, cool, or neutral tones. A particular skin tone looks good with a selected colour family. For example, a person with a cool skin tone usually looks good in blues and pinks. But here's the catch. A person with a cool skin tone might not look good in all shades of blue. A navy blue can look drab on a person while an electric blue can look fabulous; similarly a peachy-pink can look drab on a person but a rosy-pink can look fab.

So be careful while choosing the colours of your apparel or make-up.

People who understand colour look more interesting, confident, self assured, and attractive. Colours affect the way you look. Right colours will make you appear bright and beautiful while wrong colours can make you look pasty and give you a flat look. Wrong colours can make you look tired, can highlight or create shadows and under-eye dark circles and even make your teeth look yellowish. Your skin might look pale as though you are ill. Oh God! This is reason enough to look for the right colours, lest we want all our efforts of looking good, go down the drain. Colour has the power to make you look healthy or unhealthy, thin or fat, short or tall.

My style book

How do you know if a particular colour is right for you?

If you wear a colour that makes:

- Your skin tone appear radiant and glowing
- Your eyes appear brighter and clearer
- Your hair reflects highlights or colour

Then you can safely choose that colour.

Always check the colour of your dress or make-up and match it to your skin tone against a mirror in natural day light. Bright yellow lights in the stores usually make everything look good. So be smart and try to take help from an attendant when you are finalising the colour. Ask them to get the stuff near a source where you can judge the product in natural light. If it is not possible, then the second best practice is to check the products in white light.

Quick Tip: Create a style book (traditional log book or e-book, your choice!). The purpose is to create a ready reference. In your free time, mix and match your various dresses and accessories; wear them and behave like a fashion model. Ask a friend to click a few snaps. Now create a book where you can paste these snaps as ready reference where you can check which colours look good on you, what make-up suits you and which dresses make you look like a style diva. In fact your friend can give her inputs too.

Cool skin tone

A cool skin tone reflects pinkish or bluish undertones. So colours that have jewel ones like blues, greens, pinks, purples, blue-greens, magentas, and blue-based eds are the best for this category. They look better in pure white than ivory. People vith a cool skin tone can wear solid colours like black without compromising on he overall look. Their foundation will have a pinkish undertone. If your skin colour eflects cool tones then go for a lipstick that has shades of ruby, garnet, shades of berry, and fuchsia-red undertones. If your complexion is on the paler side, try to use softer pigments unless you want to give yourself a gothic and a dramatic look. The colour palatte for them is:

COLOURS FOR COOL SKIN TONE

white	pale green	electric blue	cool pink
light grey	pale yellow	cool turquoise	hot pink
grey	aqua	chinese blue	magenta
charcoal grey	ice violet	lemon yellow	fuchsia
black	ice pink	light green	royal blue
pale beige	ice blue	green	burgundy
navy blue	baby pink	emerald green	bluish red
blue	silver	pine green	deep red

Black is beautiful but that doesn't mean that you always have to wear black from head to toe to look slimmer. As long as a colour suits you, any colour if worn from head to toe will give you the same slimming effect.

Monochrome dressing (dressing in one colour from head to toe) is all about looking slimmer and taller. So go for colours which make you look bright and then dress yourself in the same colour.

If you have a cool skin tone, an eggplant purple will give you the same effect. If you are warm toned, a boiled egg yolk grey can give you the same effect. If you are neutral, khaki will make you look taller and slimmer.

Let us find out some more about the various colour palette for each type of skin tone. Look at these carefully. These are just rough guidelines when you choose colours, but do remember to put any apparel next to your skin in natural daylight before you give it a final nod. Once you feel that a particular colour makes you feel good and looks bright on you, only then zero-in on it. It's better to have a few good fitting, bright-coloured pieces than a messy wardrobe that will simply lie useless. Select carefully so that you can wear the pieces as often as possible. Team them up with the right accessories to create the most alluring dressing experience.

Brown

Red Beige

Grey

Green Purple

Blue

Warm skin tone

Warm skin tones reflect peach or golden. So the colours which have earthy tones like yellows, oranges, browns, yellowish-greens, and orange-based reds are best suited for this category. They look better in ivory white than pure white. Look washed out with colours like black if worn near the face. Your foundation will have a yellowish undertone. If you are warm toned, then look for a lipstick which has brick, copper, wine, and coral-red undertones. Golden accessories and golden eye-shadow both look great on them. They can create a glam diva look with a red pout and a soft golden hue of a bronzer to combat the yellowness of their skin. The colour palette for them is:

COLOURS FOR WARM SKIN TONE

apple white	yellow	orange	olive
beige	mustard yellow	orangish red	grey
light brown	pumpkin yellow	brownish red	light jade
chocolate	terracota	tomato red	dark green
mahogany	rust	lime green	turquoise
camel brown	peach	leaf green	teal
golden yellow	salmon pink	yellowish green	lilac
bronze	pure white	moss green	gold

Neutral skin tone

Neutral skin tone reflects olive green, pale yellow, or bluish brown colours. So colours that go well with this skin tone are oranges, olive greens, electric blues, greys, and all pastel colours. They look washed out in either pure white or black. Their foundation will be neutral. If you have a neutral skin tone, look for orange or brown undertones for your lip wear. Contrary to popular belief, neutrals can wear a wide range of colours and they look good in them too. Most of the Asians, Afro-Americans, and Latinas fall under this category. They look good in pastel shades and should avoid very dark colours in make-up. The neutrals have the advantage that they can easily look sultry with very little effort only if they put on the correct make-up. Lilac and moss green eye-shadows look the best on these people. Clear lipstick or gloss looks better on them than dark matte lipstick. The colour palette for them is:

COLOURS FOR NEUTRAL SKIN TONE

white	light blue	pale yellow	lavender
pale beige	sky blue	pale pink	mauve
cocoa	blue	pastel pink	light mauve
copper brown	pastel blue	pink	raspberry
greyish blue	aqua blue	rose pink	fig
bluish grey	pastel green	bluish pink	plum
slate grey	bluish green	watermelon red	dark navy
navy grey	emerald green	burgundy	silver

Chapter Four

Dress as per the occasion

Appropriate dressing means wearing something according to your age and as per the occasion

We already know the importance of dressing as per one's age. Dressing stylishly doesn't mean that you dress up like a teen queen. Appropriate dressing means wearing something according to your age and as per the occasion. Yes! You heard it right. Dressing yourself as per the occasion is absolutely important. A person appearing shabbily in torn jeans and a roughed up T-shirt is bound to fail in an interview. A person wearing a stark red dress in a funeral will be looked upon as a complete freak. A bride would never wear black as her bridal dress. So we see that it is really important to dress as per the occasion.

Formal dress

Dressing for office

Formal

Formal dressing is followed in almost all the corporate sectors. Women don't find it very difficult to dress formally if they know how to team up a shirt and a trouser with a closed-toe shoe. Here are some of the rules that should be followed for the best and most appropriate power dressing at the office.

Go for business suits if required. Nothing beats a well-tailored business suit. You can also wear well-fitting blouses or formal shirts with pencil skirts or formal A-line skirts and trousers. Closed-toe shoes are a must. Shoes can be heels or flats. Avoid flashy colours such as an all-neon suit. However, a splash of colour in a scarf is appropriate.

Accessories such as jewellery must be simple and traditional.

Piercing anywhere besides earrings for women (one in each ear) must be removed. Tattoos too should not be visible.

Hair should be well-cut and carefully styled. No messy hairdos or neon highlights.

Wear light make-up, choose subtle colours, and avoid sparkles, baubles, or flashy colours.

Your bag should look formal too. Usually black and brown mid-size bags go well with business wear.

Business casual

Business casual has a wide array of choices but is often wrongly interpreted. Be very careful when dressing in business casuals; as this is a different kind of dressing than for a party or a coffee meeting.

Clothing should be conservative, well fitting, and nice. Button-down shirts, trousers, blouses, dresses, sport coats, and skirts are suitable. Clothes should be ironed. Casual clothes don't mean that you can wear them right out from the dryer.

Shoes need not be patent-leather and polished; loafers or similar styles are acceptable.

Avoid sneakers and sandals, and in most cases closed-toed shoes for women are still required.

However, styles can vary towards more trendy looks like peep-toe shoes or wedge heels. Keep skirts knee-length or longer. Avoid trousers that

Business casual dress

fall till the knee; they should be either three-quarters in length or full length. Jeans and belts should not have a lot of embellishments. Keep it simple. Showing a lot of skin (like a bare midriff, or too much cleavage) is definitely a no-no.

Avoid sweats, cut-offs, tank tops, and flip-flops.

Pair jeans with pleasant shirts like polo shirts or casual button-downs. A T-shirt is sometimes acceptable, if it is in good condition. Avoid T-shirts with slogans or ads for things such as beer companies, to office.

Don't go overboard with make-up. It should be conservative; after all you are still going to office.

You can carry a fancy tote as long as it is not too dominating on your overall look. Moderately stylish with less embellishments and studs will look good with a business casual.

Dressing for funereal and memorial ceremonies

An emotional environment like funereal and memorial ceremonies leave many in a state of confusion. They are not sure what to wear and how to behave. Many avoid going to such occasions. Here are a few tips for dressing down for such ceremonies.

Keep it sober and classic. Wearing white or black is a norm in various cultures

Funeral and memorial service wear

around the world. But if you don't have these mourning dresses, wear anything which is sober and natural. Off-white, beige, khakis, and light browns are equally good if you do not have pure white.

Do not wear anything bright. You can wear a dress as long as the colour isn't bright or wildly patterned.

In many cultures, red is a colour for festivals and would be inappropriate for a funeral. Generally, play it safe with any dark or subdued colour.

Do not show a lot of skin. Keep it for your romantic dates. Try to wear something modest that covers you well.

Do not wear make-up. If you really can't do without make-up, then put a bit of tinted moisturizer and a bit of lip balm. In emotional moments usually make-up gets washed off with tears and sweat. And you will also look washed off and creepy with a layer of drained out make-up in such ceremonies.

Jewellery should be kept to minimal or nil. You will get other occasions to show off your new diamond set.

Wear shoes which are flat and sober. You might have to move around a lot and that too on a damp and muddy ground. You might have to take off your shoes often so no high heel stilettos for such ceremonies.

Do not carry a fancy oversized shopper for such occasions. Keep your bag simple which is able to carry your lip balm, eye wear, tissues, money bag, and a phone. That's all that you would require for such ceremonies.

Dressing for holidays

We love this part of the year. For many, holidays are in winters, especially around Christmas and New Year and for a few it is summers. You might like to pack the whole world when it comes to holiday packing. Here are a few pointers to help you take only the best pieces.

If you are going for a summer holiday, you will require all your beach dresses and light clothing. If you are going to colder parts of the world, you should be well equipped with coats, jackets, and boots to counter the extreme weather. Therefore, plan according to your destination.

Summer holidays would mean a lot of beachwear, t-dresses, shorts and miniskirts, or cotton wears and hosiery pieces. Choose accordingly and pack the ones that you plan to wear. Colder parts would require you to keep warm, so do not forget body warmers, gloves, hats or caps, scarves, stoles, etc.

Holidays will also include a bit of partying. So keep the basics ready. An LBD or a shimmery skirt teamed with a well-fitted top, a sparkly dress, should be kept ready with some statement jewellery like elegant and modern cocktail rings, dangling earrings in unique design, necklaces that are bold and colourful, and bracelets that call attention to your wrist.

Holiday dressing

Don't be afraid of colour. And don't be afraid to wear big. Just remember if you wear an oversized ring, go minimal on the other jewellery.

Get walking shoes and flip-flops ready if you are going to a summer destination and warm boots ready for winter destination. You can also pack peep-toe courts or gladiator stilettos for any party that you might attend.

Go for a bolder than usual natural look. Try a smoky eye or a red lip. The thing to remember is if you go for more make-up on the eye, go for a more natural shade for your lips and vice versa. Don't forget the flushed cheeks. Try a peach shade of blush on the apples of your cheeks. If you are going to a summer destination, do not forget your bronzer. And follow sun-block cream like religion.

Pack a beach bag if you are going to a summer destination. Else a sling bag is perfect. It's handy to carry essentials like passport, currency, a bit of make-up, phone, a map, and an address book in your sling bag. You can wear an across body sling bag to a party as well if it is a little fancy.

Dressing for a dinner party

Everyone loves to get invites for dinner parties by friends and families. But the confusion arises when the invitation comes from a person not well-known to you, like your new boss, a client, or an office colleague. Yes! Parties are meant to glam up but if the host is not that known then you should play it down. The best bet is to go for a classic and elegant look.

Cocktail dress

Take a good look at your invitation. You can tell a lot about the expected tone of dressing in the dinner party. You may find instructions stating "Casual" or "Formal" or "Cocktail Attire" which can direct your wardrobe choices. Speak to the host of the party a couple of days beforehand if you are in doubt about how you are expected to dress for the event.

Except for the most informal of dinner parties, such as BBQs or picnics, jeans and shorts are generally not acceptable attire when invited for a dinner party.

Wherever "Business attire" is indicated, wear matching pant suits or skirt suits to the dinner party. Wherever "Cocktail attire" is indicated, bring out your cocktail dress and gowns. An evening dress with a light jacket or an arm covering is acceptable for regular dinner parties.

Wear comfortable heels. Too high and you will be uncomfortable moving around. The shoes can be peep toes or a gladiator cut. Avoid rugged boots to such occasions. The element of elegance should also reflect in your shoes and the way you walk.

Carry a small bag, clutch, or a cocktail bag to such events. Clutches are versatile as they can be used in various occasions. Take care not to choose a very shimmery and glossy bag for business dinners.

Keep the make-up elegant too. Too dark or glam make-up should be reserved only for New Year parties or marriage ceremonies. For business dinners keep the make-up simple yet pronounced. For cocktail parties you can opt for not-so-dark smoky eyes and nude lips.

Quick tip: When in doubt, pick your LBD or a black traditional saree. Women can always fall back on that wardrobe staple of the LBD. From summer through winter, for indoor and outdoor events, a black dress that fits well will look appropriate at most events, no matter how formal or informal. If you're still in doubt, choose a formal saree with less or no embellishments for such occasions. Don't wear chiffon or see-through light fabric. Wear something which is suitable to the occasion.

Dressing for an evening out or coffee meet

A movie date, a coffee meet, a garden party, or an afternoon event at the racecourse; these are occasions that crop up time and again in everyone's life. And don't we all love to dress up for such occasions! A casual environment doesn't mean that you dress shabbily. Just because you are meeting up with friends or known acquaintances doesn't mean you can go in your shorts and flip-flops. Plan appropriately and you might pep up the meeting with your saucy and sexy look.

Keep the colour of the fabric light and the pattern of dress floral and prints. You can never go wrong with floral designs, and the classic cut of a sheath or a halter dress with a fitted bodice and flowing skirt for an afternoon event.

You can also opt for off-white, khaki or any light pastel shade of pinks and blues for such occasions. If you are wearing a dress, team it up with a hat.

If you are planning to wear denims for a coffee meet or evening out with friends, team it up with a nice floral top or shirt. A good denim short or skirt will look great with a printed halter top. If you are wearing denim trousers, team it up with printed T-shirts or tunic dresses or kurtis.

You don't have to look dramatic because you are going out for a movie. Keep the make-up minimal or rather casual. During daytime, never wear dark make-up. Go for a pink or peach flushed look.

Coffee meet dress

Bring out your casual wedges or comfortable heels. Keep the stilettos only for parties. Flats and classic pumps are also a good option.

Carry your oversized tote and sunglasses. This is the ideal time to flaunt those cherished pieces.

There are several other occasions where one wonders of the correct way to present oneself. The list here is endless. Though only a few puzzling ones have been listed here; an open mind and clear understanding about a particular situation can help you dress well.

Dressing is an art. Akin to a well-decorated home or a beautifully done up place, dressing oneself gives a similar kind of satisfaction. Moreover, dressing is an expression of your creativity.

A well-dressed person is always cherished and is considered an icon. We always look up to style divas for fashion predictions. Perhaps this is because each one of us wants to look as good as them. They look nice in a particular outfit but the same cannot be said about you. Don't get me wrong; all I am saying is that don't allow yourself to follow the trends blindly. Evaluate yourself and then take inspiration from these style icons to choose what will look good on you.

Chapter Five

Style sins

What's wrong with my style?

Oh! How I wish everyone could be a style diva. We all think once in a while about the statement 'what's wrong with my style?' Well, we all make a few mistakes every now and then and become an eye sore for many. We feel that there is nothing wrong with the way we dress but onlookers find our dressing tacky and frumpy. A few have the 'I don't care' attitude about what others think, but there are still those who want to comply with the onlooker's barometer. The point is, if you are spending so much time and energy in dressing up; then it ought to be perfect. Here's a list of a few style sins which we must avoid at all costs.

Wearing ill-fitting churidaars with short kurtis

Getting a salwar suit material stitched gives us the luxury of a perfect fit. But usually women ask their tailors to keep enough room around their thighs in their churidaars. Too tight and the stitches start falling apart but if the fit is loose around the thighs and if it is worn with a short kurti, it lends more weight and shapelessness to your legs giving you a shabby look. If you do not have a good tailor who can give you a good fit, opt for hosiery tights or leggings. These days leggings and jeggings are more popular with short kurtis or shirt dresses. Or you can opt for strong and synthetic fabric which can withhold the stitches in a fitted churidaar.

Ill-fitting churidaar

Wearing Anarkali kurtis

That is the biggest fashion faux pas and does nothing to enhance your body shape if you are not tall and slim. It looks more like a tent where you can hide your body bumps. Avoid wearing Anarkali kurtis at all cost; the only exception would be if you are pregnant. Few women team it up with jeans. Please ladies! You will do a big favour to yourself if you kept the kurtis short and tunic style with your jeans. Or else opt for shapely A-line kurtis for a more defined shape. Keep the length modest if you have heavy thighs.

Anarkali kurtis

Long chunnis

Wearing very long chunnis or duppatas

Many love to flaunt metres of long dupatta over there stitched Indian suits. The flowing garment looks more of a nuisance. It doesn't add any value to the overall look of the ensemble. Uncomfortable and impractical is what can be termed for oversized chunnis or duppatas. They are unmanageable and usually get entangled at various places. For sure you won't look like a Bollywood screen siren with an extra long duppata. All they do is make you look shorter than what you really are.

Wearing Jaipuri jutis with a pair of jeans

I love 'Jaipuri jutis'. The best part about them is that you don't have to ponder if the left foot or right foot has been worn correctly. You can wear either of the shoes on any of your feet. They look great with ethnic wear, but look tacky with a pair of jeans and a top. Wear shoes that are more appropriate with your casual wear. Jaipuri Jutis with jeans are an absolute no-no.

Jaipuri jutis

Lazy dressing

Dirty, broken finger nails, chipped nail polish, messy hair, messy look with dirty shoes and clothing, are all signs of a lazy person. Don't be so demotivated when it comes to your look and clothing. Being well-groomed and sporting a clean look are signs of hygiene, much appreciated both at work and at home. Wear your own size. Try out the dresses before you buy them. All shops don't necessarily have the same sizing. You might fit into a 'medium size' in one shop and into a 'large size' in another. If you try to fit into a smaller size, it will just highlight your rolls of fat in all the wrong places. The very tight hipster pant, where the stomach and love handles spill over and out of the garment, topped by a very short top, can leave the exposed stomach looking ghastly. Make sure you buy your trousers large enough and that your tops are long enough to cover your middle in style.

Chipped nail polish

Also keep an eye on any underarm sweat stain or other stains on your clothes. Don't wear clothes with stains as they look unappealing. The same goes for shoes. Keep them cleaned, polished, and tidy.

Wearing sweatshirts, sweatpants, track pants, and hoodies

Many find dressing up way too time-consuming. Many attach lot of importance to comfort dressing that they walk out in their pyjamas to the nearest store. They wear crushed velvet track suits and sneakers; throw in a designer or oversized handbag on their elbow with some giant sunglasses and think that they look good. But the reality is that they look totally unattractive. Few others carry a messier look by wearing sweatpants and stained hoodies outside. Sweatpants are for working out. Moreover, sweatpants are for sleeping in or for wearing around your house while you vacuum – not for wearing to a mall.

Sweatshirts

Large baggy clothes

Wearing large baggy clothes and undergarments

Large baggy clothing (especially shirts, baggy T-shirts, and jumpers) can make everyone look larger than they actually are. They look good on no one. Fitted clothes (not skin tight), no matter what your size, are far more flattering and give you a slim look. And please don't resort to wearing leggings with a baggy T-shirt or jumper, unless you would like to look like a meatball on a skewer. Wear the underwear of your size. Too large and you might end up looking like your grandma; too small and you might develop bulges in and around your bosom.

Wearing visible bra straps under halter dresses and tank tops

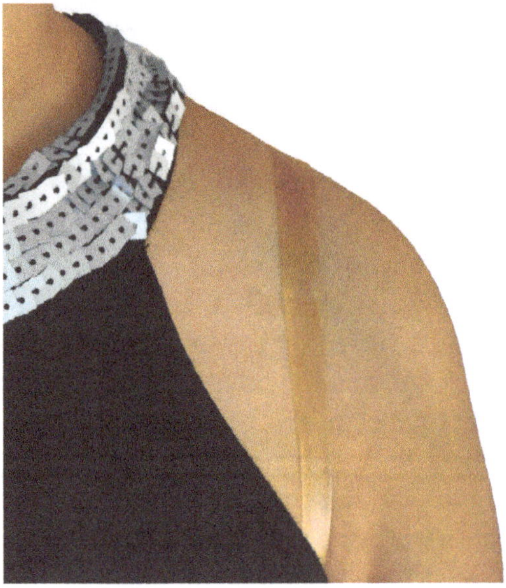

Visible bra straps

Visible bra straps under halter necks, razor backs, or tank tops looks very edgy. Your look gets completely killed thanks to these. They might be the transparent ones but still they make you look sloppy instead of sexy. Avoid it at all cost; instead try wearing a skinny-strap tank top with a razor-back bra, or strapless bra, and layer your tank top with a second tank top.

Wearing Capri pants with socks and sneakers

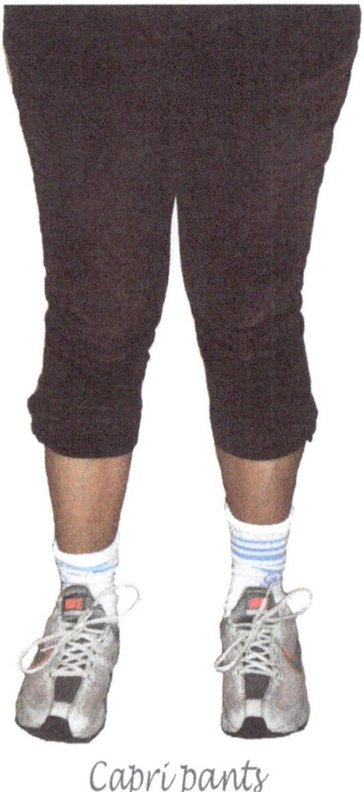

Capri pants

Oh! Lord, nothing could be more ghastly a sight than wearing socks with three quarter pants and that too with running shoes or sneakers. Ladies! Bear in mind that socks do not add any beauty to your overall look. It might have been fine as a school girl, but as a woman, try and show your shapely ankles rather than hiding them behind socks and in case you want to wear them, do cover them up with full length trousers and closed shoes. Should you choose the above combination, let me warn you that this is a lethal combination; one that will make you look short, fat, and frumpy. If you need practicality and comfort, try cushioned flip-flops with your Capri or a wedge heel instead of running shoes.

Hot pants or shorts

If you have shapely and toned legs, flaunt them in hot pants but only during your summer vacations or for a beach-side trip. Hot pants suit a collegiate and not a woman in her 30s. Shorts (especially the cut-off jean short variety) are tacky and cheap beyond your kitchen garden. Too short and you might risk looking like you are living in your teens. If you have cellulite or bulky thighs, please cover them up in decent length shorts. Try an above-the-knee cotton skirt or walking shorts for going out.

Hot pants

White pants

Wearing white pants with pronounced pockets and colourful underwear

Many love to wear a pair of crisp white pants along with a nice kaftan style top. While shopping for white trousers most women don't pay attention to the fabric of these pants. Sometimes the fabric is so light and sheer that pockets of these trousers take centre stage. This is what everyone will notice first when you wear a white pant with sheer fabric. In case you would want to wear a white pant with light fabric, make sure that the pockets are taken out by professional tailor for a much cleaner look. Also, wear skin coloured underpants for sporting a clean, seamless look.

Wearing rubber sandals with your jeans

Rubber sandals are comfortable. They are made for wadding through water or mud. They are also specially designed to wear on dew-laden grass. You guessed it right; these are for your garden or backyard or perhaps even for a walk on the beach. But many women love to wear these to supermarkets along with their denims. Wear them around the garden, the pool, the seaside or cottage, but don't wear them out grocery shopping or to a movie or anywhere else.

These bright, rubber shoes look childish by all means. You don't want to look like a child parading around, do you?

Rubber sandals

Wearing nude hose with sandals and wearing the wrong coloured hose

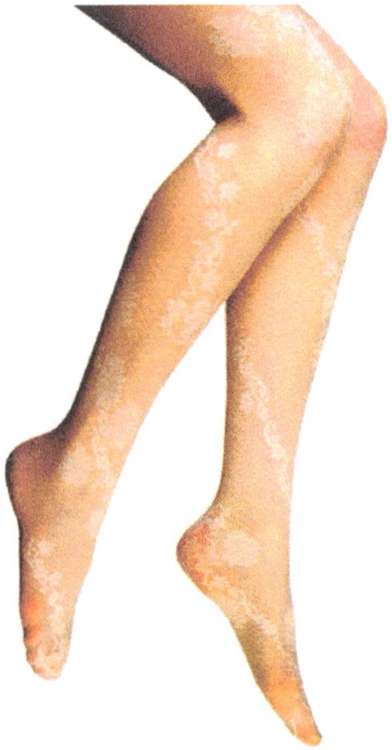

Nude hose with sandals

Office-going women want to wear skirts but the minute they decide to wear a nude hose with an open-toed sandal, they commit the biggest style sin. Nothing looks tackier than a nude hose with open- toed sandals. Make sure that the hose is in perfect shape without any cuts or nips. You'll look taller and trimmer by matching the colour of your hose to your shoes and your hem. Wearing a black skirt and shoes? Opt for sheer black hose. Have a bright blue dress and taupe shoes? Go for the taupe-coloured hose. If you only wear a black hose because they hide things you don't want people to see then you are making a big mistake. Unless your whole outfit's black, you're calling attention to your legs.

Wearing wrong length trouser with heels

Always keep the length of your trousers and jeans in the format of three. All hemmed to different lengths for flats, heels, and sandals. Whatever heel length you may choose, make sure that your pants are long enough to avoid the look that makes you appear as if you are 'waiting for the floods.' Many women these days do not realise that a boot-cut or any other style of jeans should only be 1/2 to 1 inch above the ground while wearing heels. People look silly when they wear heels (especially in boots) with trousers of imperfect lengths.

Trousers with heels

Skirts

Wearing wrong length skirts

Skirts are eminent dress pieces, especially in the urban working woman's wardrobe. But a wrong length skirt can spoil the look one might be trying to achieve. A wrong length skirt can make you look fat, shorter than you really are, or simply unappealing. While choosing a skirt always keep in mind your height and weight. A horizontally-tiered skirt will make short legs look stumpy. This style should ideally be worn by tall, slim women with long legs. If you're short, choose skirts with vertical lines. To slim wide legs, go for hems that end either above or below the fullest part of the calf but not directly on it.

Wearing mirrors and feathers

Mirrors and feathers add a fun element; not a professional appearance. So if it's not a fancy dress competition, refrain from wearing mirrors and feathers. There are but a handful of things that look good only on the gypsies. So please do not emulate gypsy fashion in your daily wear. If you have invested in any such piece, just keep it as a memento.

Mirrors and feathers

Headgear

Wearing a loud or wrong headgear

Headgear is meant to be accessorise your entire outfit. Also, it helps in solving the purpose of other practical needs like saving your head from the heat of the sun or helping your head in braving extreme cold weather. Many a times, headgear is too overbearing or loud that it looks like a fire fighter's helmet. Wear floral bands in a subtle way. Your hat should compliment your entire outfit and not stand out on its own. Monkey caps are an absolute no-no. Please find other alternatives to save yourself from cold weather. All in all, it would make you look like a terrorist. Also avoid grandma's woollen head scarves or woven woollen scarves as these are scary. Leave it aside for your mum or the older ladies.

Wearing too much jewellery

Women love jewellery. This is true in some parts of India, where jewellery is a status symbol and the best way to flaunt it is to wear every single piece at one go. Should you choose to look like a Christmas tree, then this is probably how you should; not otherwise. Jewellery is merely an addition to your persona, so don't let it overrule your personality. Jewellery accessories should therefore be kept simple and minimal. Match it with your dress and wear it as per the occasion. Until and unless it's your own marriage, try and highlight only one piece. If you are wearing a statement necklace, play down on earrings and bracelets. If you are wearing a cocktail ring, make sure that there are no other prominent rings on your other fingers.

Jewellery

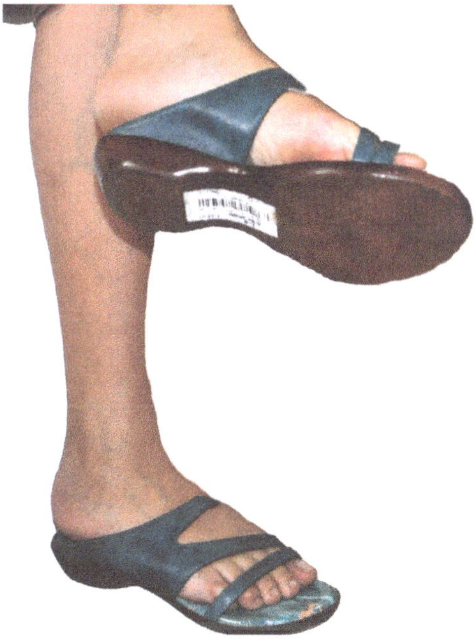

Stickers left on shoes

Remove the labels from dresses and shoes

Labels and stickers left on shoes are a glaring sign depicting that you are either too demotivated or too lazy. The 'D & G' shades that you may have recently purchased need not be put on the exhibition with the label gracing the product. Please peel it off. The price tag or label on your dress needs to be removed too. You don't want to show off the price you paid for that piece or the brand you prefer. And don't forget the price sticker under your shoes. Many women like to put it on display. Ladies, please understand, nobody wants to know the brand of your shoes or its price, so please remove it before using them.

Wearing very chunky army boots or heels

Chunky heels look good on but a few. There are women who borrow their boyfriend's boots or shoes from uncles who have served the army with a view to team them up with a pair of jeans or trousers. Trust me they look tacky and unpleasant. Please understand that the so-called rough-tough look gives out a wrong message. You might have been a tomboy in your teens but you don't necessarily have to behave like one now. Get boots or pumps meant for all terrains; ones that manage to retain femininity. Clean and stylish shoes are important in defining your style.

Chunky army boots

Hanger loops sticking out of your dress

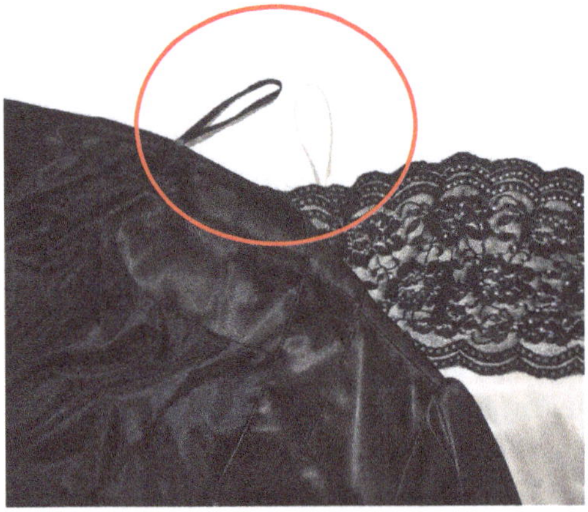

Hanger loops

Those slim loops created on either side of a top or dress is meant to help the shopkeepers display the piece elegantly on a hanger. Once you have bought a piece, their purpose is redundant. So snip them off ladies. Don't let them hang out unnecessarily on a party evening. It looks absolutely distasteful if those thin ribbons or loops pop out of your underarm area. Cut them with scissors, or remove them carefully without damaging the stitches. Trust me, you won't miss having them on your dress.

As we see that there is huge list of style sins that many of us forego. Bear in mind that these are just a few common mistakes that we make in our day-to-day lives. If we are careful, we can avoid these and look our best. A good looking and stylish person is always admired by peers and viewed as an icon. So consider your dressing style as a way to influence people. In fact, many HR personnel in companies keep a close watch on the list of most popular employees. They are always considered first for promotion before others (obviously there are other factors like performance appraisal, but this proves as an added advantage). A well-groomed and stylish person can be successful in easily winning the admiration of her colleagues. They are largely considered as leaders in their own way.

Chapter Six

Magic underwears

Figure-forming underwear achieves instant results by taking care of all un-shapely lumps and flab

Good underwear is everyone's delight. Yes! While it is delightful for the wearer as they get the comfort and the compliments; it is also a delight for the onlooker as they can avoid witnessing ghastly and un-shapely lumps of fat. Special knickers or control pants, tights, body shapers and enhanced bras come handy where nature has not been too generous. Figure-forming underwear achieves instant results by taking care of all un-shapely flab.

Underwear isn't something that you can take lightly as they are equally resourceful in getting you the perfect look. Just because it is worn underneath, doesn't mean that it has any less relevance than your other clothes. It is quite tempting to think that 'No one is going to see it so why bother.' These garments can often be spotted through your fabric. A good bra and pants can do wonders for your look. They can radically change the shape of a body.

Most women ruin their look with an ill-fitting bra. The most common mistake we all make is wearing a bra that is too small in the cup or too loose around the body, for instance a 34B instead of 32D, or a 38C instead of a 36DD.

This not only gives poor support and causes bulging necklines and lumps under fitted tops, but it can also lead to skin irritation and bad posture and sometimes cause the underwire to pinch into the delicate breast tissue. In the correct bra, not only are your breasts properly supported, but your torso looks longer with a better posture. Finding the right bra shape and, more importantly, the right size can be a life-changing experience. Until you find your correct fitting bra, you can't imagine how good it looks and feels.

Manufacturers developed the bra sizing system over a period of 70 years. Besides, our understanding of the system has changed drastically as body shapes and sizes have changed in this course of time. Furthermore, it was never designed for larger cup sizes. The classic bra sizing system was designed for cup sizes between A to D. We now have cups that scale up to size JJ. Thus we can easily conclude that looking for a perfect fit is quite a daunting task when it comes to choosing from amongst various brands that are not very clear about the sizing and do not follow a universal sizing pattern. Keep an open eye when choosing for the right fit.

Do you wear a faded T-shirt, or a torn jumper, or a broken heel? Then why do you wear unshapely, under or oversized, frayed underwear? All underwear that are discoloured, have frayed elastic, have skin digging straps, with wires poking out, with lace coming off, or are ill fitting, need to get off your drawer. You just can't wear them and damage yourself. Instead get underwear that supports and shapes your lady lumps perfectly. Underwear is a long time necessary investment. So make these investments carefully and choose the right bra or pants to enhance your shape. Try and get good quality products that will last long. They might be expensive but they are certainly worth the value.

Pants

Get the pants of your size. Don't feel ashamed to ask for the right fit even if that means asking for a larger size. If you wear a smaller size, it is quite likely that the fabric will dig into your skin and create gashes and rashes. I am sure no one likes to mess up their sensitive area with painful rashes. You might also want to double check your bottom if you wear very tight underpants, the fabric will dig into your bottom to create an illusion of double cheek. And mind you, it will be visible through your skirts and

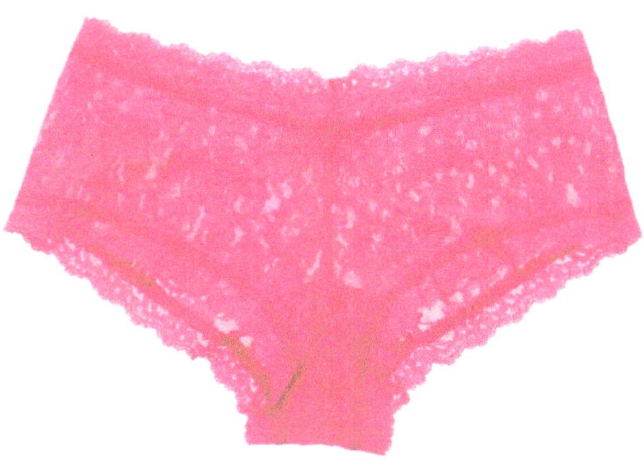

trousers and be a ghastly sight for others, leave aside your own self. In doing so, you might also highlight your love handles.

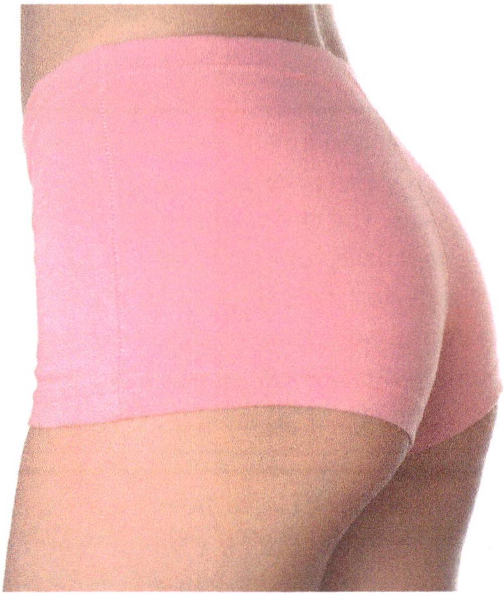

Keep G-strings only for your bedrooms. Lacy G-strings peeping out of your low waists look like absolute trash. You want to look class apart and not the kind who is falling apart.

If you have a flabby tummy, you need pants with waist bands that reach up to your rib cage. These pants have industrially strengthened elastic that holds all flab in shape and when stretched until the rib cage, avoids the spillage of flab at the wrong place. The elastic secures itself along the rib cage.

Husbands and boyfriends might mock you and call it a tummy holder. But you know what best it can do to your look with the instant tummy tucking.

If you are keen to wear cotton pants, avoid wearing bikini briefs. They look good only on supermodels. Get regular fits that can be pulled up to your belly button and will keep your lower belly shapely and smooth.

If you have large thighs and saddle bags, wear control pants which have an extra thick layer of Lycra around the thigh and waist area. This will redistribute the flab around bum and thigh and give you a slimmer and smoother appearance around that area.

If you have a saggy posterior or bottom with cellulite showing from beneath your trousers, you will need contouring knickers which have a built-in lift. Such contouring knickers cover any skin imperfections and the thinnest of fabric can slide on it effortlessly, giving you a smoother look. Latex, bum-lifting shapers, or knickers can give you the required shapeliness around your butt.

If you want to create an illusion of a waist, then an all-in-one body suit will help you achieve this. A body suit doesn't let the flab spill out from anywhere. Though tiresome to get in, you would feel the difference if you believe that this would make your middle look perfect. Be sure that the one you wear is of your size and of good quality. An all-in-one body suit should be made up of good quality nylon so that the fabric of the clothes worn over it doesn't cling onto it; rather it should give you a smooth and slim finish. Should you find the perfect match in all-in-one body suit, you are bound to get the perfect look that was long ago only achieved with a corset.

Bra

If you have big breasts, then you ought to get a plus-size fit. Lingerie for plus size women is available along with bras designed for women with bigger breasts. These give a good support to the breasts while defining the torso. Anyone above the cup size 'D' needs to wear a well-fitted bra with good support. Avoid the extra baggage of laces and decoration and opt for a smooth finish. Your focus should be to keep the volume down. Underwiring in such cases is a must as it will give you the necessary support.

If you have small breasts you need to invest in a Wonder bra. The ability to increase internal padding and control of the fit with the help of strings makes it apt for women who seek some cleavage. A push-up bra too is good for women who want some more volume.

If you have sagging breasts then you need a balcony fit bra. This design helps in cupping the breast in the right places, giving it the much required lift. If your breasts are elevated at the right height, your waist looks slimmer. Overall, you look more shapely and thinner.

If you have a fat and flabby back, use a wide strapped bra that will evenly distribute the weight of your cup holders over a wide area. This will prevent the straps from digging into the flesh.

Quick Tip: Never make the mistake of wearing a white bra under a white shirt. Always wear a skin-coloured bra under a white shirt. You want a seamless look and not a defined bra line under your white shirt.

As we have spoken about the benefits of a well-fitted bra, let us find out how it feels when you have the right one.

Correct fitting bra (front)

- The centre front sits flat against the body.
- The underwire sits flat against the rib cage.
- The breast tissue is completely encased in an under wire.
- The underwire follows the natural crease of the breast.
- The cup fits snugly without bulging or gaping at the top.

Correct fitting bra (back)

- Both straps are parallel or slightly V shaped at the back.
- The band is level all the way round, without riding up at the back.
- The under band gives you a good fit.
- Straps don't dig into the shoulders.

Thus we can conclude that underwear is equally important in shaping up our bodies as well as shaping up our lives. Never neglect this aspect of your dressing. Invest in good, well-fitting pieces and you can benefit from them. No one is born with a perfect body, but it is in our hands to create a beautiful one with the help of good innerwear.

Chapter Seven

Choosing a haircut according to your face shape

Perfect cut for a perfect face! A good haircut can make a lot of difference in the way you look

A lot about your look is defined by the structure of your hair and the cut you sport. A wrong haircut can age you and the right one can bounce off a few years.

Hairstyles are predominately about shape and geometry. It's all about putting the perfect frame around a person's face to balance and bring perspective to the overall shape. The purpose is to minimise the flaws and accentuate the best features. A good hairstylist will just know instinctively what shape will or won't suit you. Knowing what will look good on your face shape will also help you communicate better with your stylist.

So choose the right haircut as per your face shape. Treat your hair with respect if you want to own beautiful and healthy coif for long.

Avoid the overuse of heating equipments and chemicals on your hair for keeping them gorgeous. Treat with deep moisturising and oiling to keep your hair looking shiny and lustrous.

As we already know of the six basic face shapes, let's find out the various hints to be borne in mind while choosing the correct haircut according to the shape of the face.

Oval shape

You are the luckiest. Any haircut will look good on you.

- ☞ For fine and longer hair, ask your stylist for soft layers throughout your hair. It will add volume and appeal to your look. If you wish to go super short, then this face structure carries the look perfectly. Ask your stylist about highlighting the hair around your face to accentuate your oval shape.
- ☞ For medium-textured or wavy hair, try a razor cut or a short bob; one that's longer at the sides and shorter at the back. This will look sexy and chic.
- ☞ Fringe options: If you have thick hair, you could go for a sexy short fringe or one that's long and blunt. For fine hair, a long wispy fringe is right for you.
- ☞ Avoid covering your facial features with heavy bangs. Don't try styles that cover up your face to an extent that they may make your face appear too elongated. Avoid short layers that add height on top of your head. Besides being dated, short layers can make your face appear long. If your hair is thick or curly, avoid a blunt cut. If you have curly hair, short hair is generally a no-no. You need to try shoulder-length or longer hair to weigh down curls.

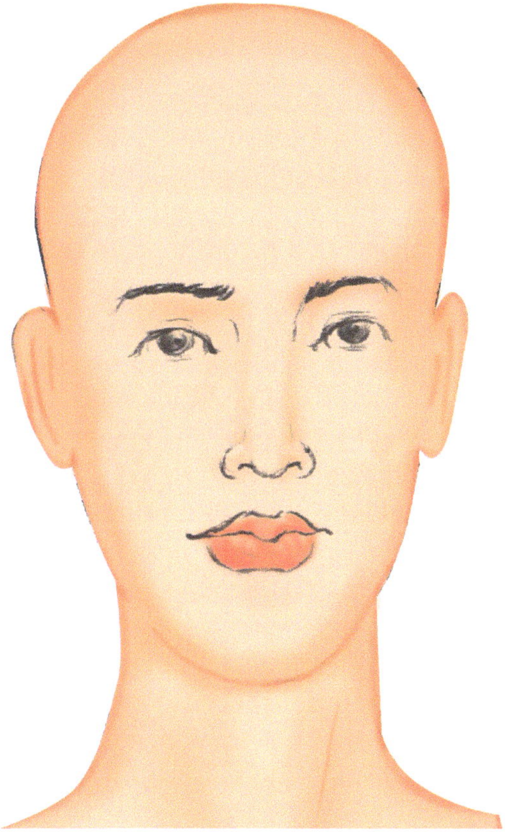

Oval shape

Heart shape

Avoid top-heavy cuts, and no one will be able to resist you. Choose a style that will create volume around the bottom of your face. But whatever your hair type, don't have your hair too long. Four inches below your shoulders is quite enough. Highlight your hair above the ears to widen your face.

- ☞ For thick long hair ask for soft layers around your chin area. Keep the layers as close to your jaw line as possible so that they can fall on your face and frame it.
- ☞ For long curly hair, keep them soft and loose. Ask the stylist to cut them round so that they lightly fall on to your face and then use a serum to keep them frizz free.
- ☞ A short bob is a safe and sexy style. It will look good on both curly as well as wavy hair; just don't let it grow any longer and supersede your jaw line. Chop out the volume around your chin. Don't go for thick, blunt, or bushy styles.
- ☞ Fringe options: A shorter, wispy fringe is low-key but will look gorgeous, especially if your hair is thick. A blunt fringe is really dramatic and will work well on all types of hair.
- ☞ Avoid short, fuller styles that emphasize the upper face or add height at the crown. Too much height at the crown will make you appear longer and narrower at the chin. Severe slicked back looks are a complete no-no. Avoid short, blunt-cut bangs and harsh, choppy layers.

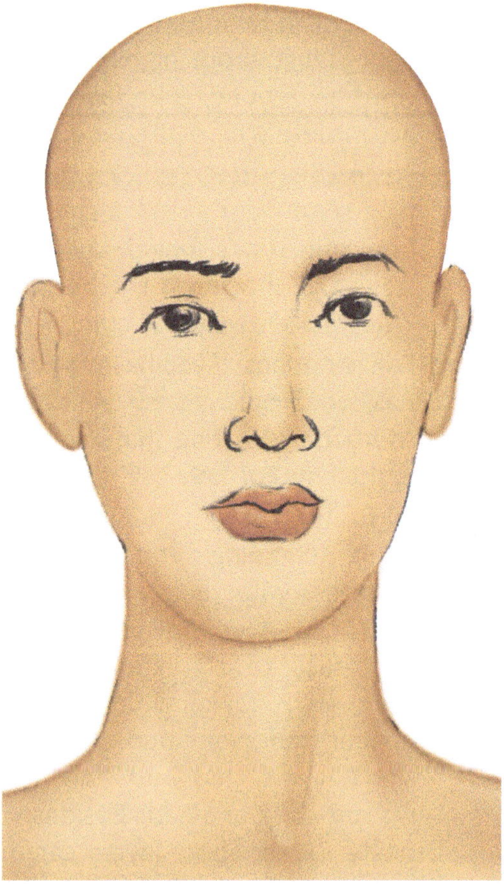

Heart shape

Triangle shape

The best style for you is the one which will balance your facial structure. A style which adds volume at the top and becomes cropped around the ears is the best for triangle shape. Don't go for very short cuts as that will make your head look smaller. Add roundness to the style and some height at the crown or deep side parted minimal bangs to look your best. Highlighting hair at the crown will add volume to your face at the top.

- ☞ For thick long hair, ask for thin soft layers around your chin but volume at the crown. A graduating bob like Mrs. Beckham is well suited for you. You can also opt for a layered mushroom shag.
- ☞ For curly hair, a crop or textured bob will look good on you. Shoulder length hairstyles are ideal for you. Just make sure that the layers do not end around your jaw line making them look wider than what they really are.
- ☞ Fringe options: Try not to sport a fringe as it will make your forehead look even smaller. Straight bushy bangs are not for you. Opt for minimal bangs that have a deep side part.
- ☞ Avoid very short hair as they make your face look very narrow at the top. Avoid fringes and bangs as they make your forehead look very small.

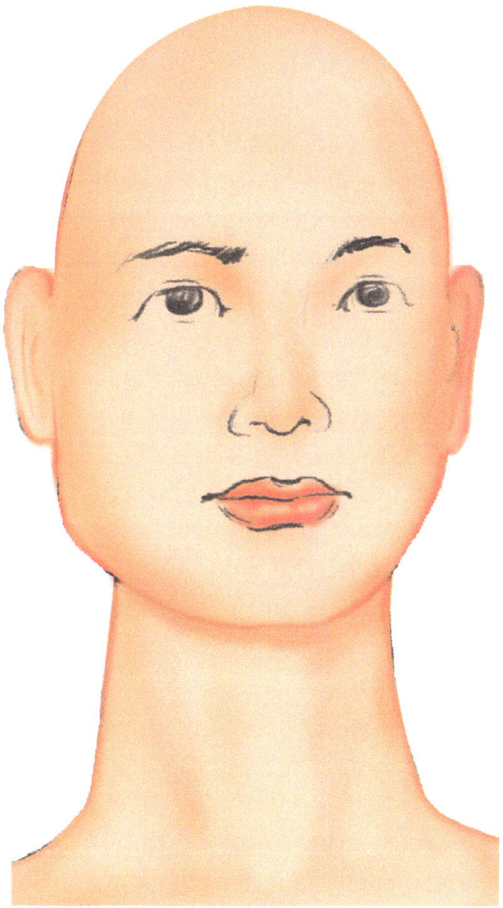

Triangle shape

Square shape

A style, which is feathered at the top and soft around your ears, is an instant disguise for a square jaw. As a rule of thumb, if a stylist suggests a cut that's above your jaw line, go elsewhere. Really short cuts will exaggerate the square-ness of your face shape. Add roundness to the style and some height at the crown or bangs to look your best. Highlighting hair all around the face will soften a square face.

- ☞ For fine hair, a long poker straight cut will be perfect and will flatter the wide jaw line. A layered bob will equally look good on you.
- ☞ For curly hair, soft textured layers around your face will soften your strong jaw line. Long hairstyles will look better on you than shoulder length or pixie styles.
- ☞ Fringe options: Most hair types, except curly, will be able to take a fringe that touches the eyebrows and one that is longer and layered at the sides. But if your hair is thick or frizzy, layer the fringe throughout to thin it.
- ☞ Avoid linear straight bangs or centre parts as they will focus on square jaw line. Avoid one-length bobs (especially chin-length) and blunt-cut bangs. These will make your face look even squarer. Highlights which frame your face around jaw area or directly end at jaw line will make your situation worse.

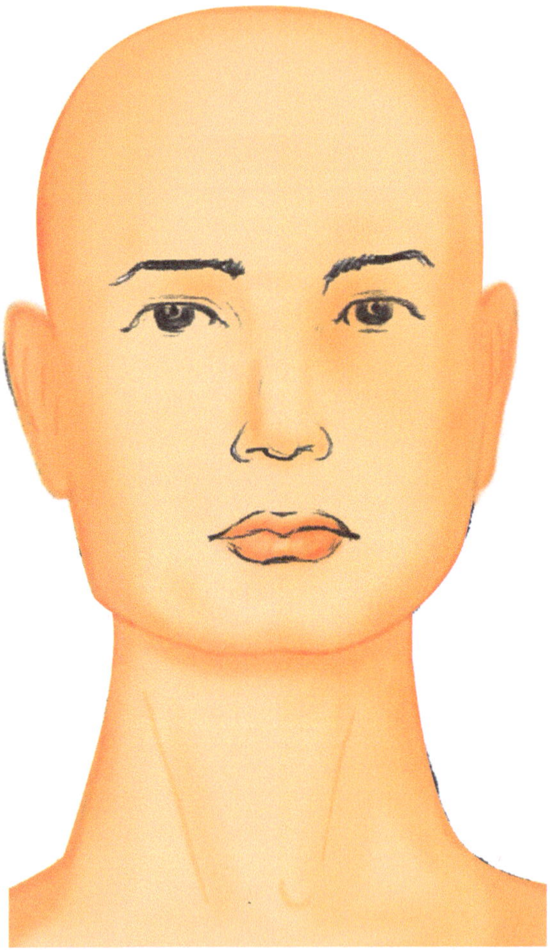

Square shape

Round shape

Contrary to popular belief, a lot of hairstyles suit a round face. A round face is soft and feminine and can be easily accentuated with various styles. Talk to your stylist about highlights at the side of the face and at the top of the head to create the illusion of length and to combat its roundedness.

- ☞ For straight hair, keep it long around your face as it will slim down your cheeks and make them look more structured. Try a graduated bob cut on to the face and higher at the back. Alternatively, a choppy shag will suit your face shape.
- ☞ For medium to long curly hair, add choppy layers through the back and the bottom of your hair to give it some shape. Keep the bob asymmetric instead of straight to avoid looking like a mushroom.
- ☞ Fringe options: Avoid a short blunt fringe as it will only emphasize a round face. On the other hand, a long wispy fringe will look great and suit fine hair. And if your hair is thicker, a longer fringe that you can sweep to the side will lengthen your face.
- ☞ Avoid chin length hair as it will add weight to your face around the cheeks. Avoid center parts, short crops, straight bangs, or any style that adds fullness around your ears as it will make your face appear wider.

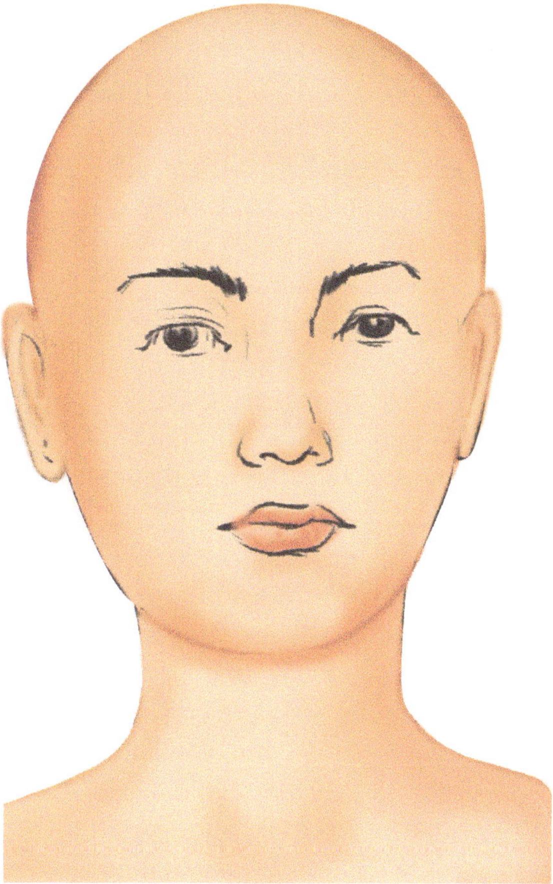

Round shape

Rectangle or oblong shape

A long face isn't all that bad. There are many ways to make it look fuller and feminine. Adding highlights to hair at the side of the face will make your face appear shorter, while keeping the forehead area darker. Consider a V-shaped style where the length is largely at the back, while the sides and front of your hair appear shorter. Also consider adding wave or curls to the hair.

- ☞ For long fine hair, go shorter with your style so that the hair looks thicker and your face looks wider around the cheeks. An unstructured layer will look good on you. Or else opt for a neat and sophisticated one length cut but make sure that your hair is not too long.
- ☞ For thick and curly hair, go for a short razor cut which is full of texture. Keep the length either shorter or longer than the shoulder length.
- ☞ Fringe options: Unfortunately in the fringe area; not all types are for your face. You could disguise a long forehead with a thick blunt-cut fringe – and you'll be surprised how feminine it makes you look. Steer clear of a fringe if you have a small forehead – it will just emphasize the length of the rest of your face.
- ☞ Avoid too much hair length as it will elongate your face even more. Avoid center parts.

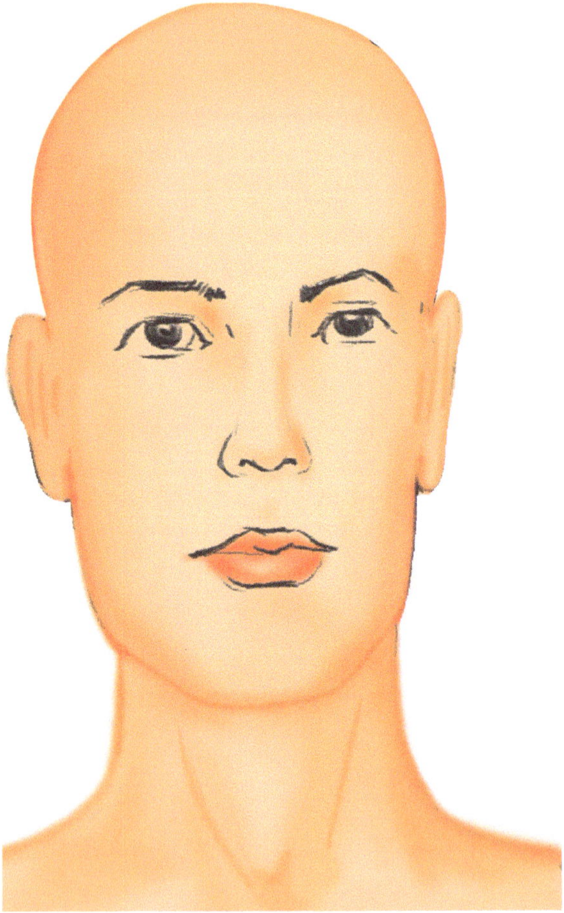

Rectangle shape

A good haircut is an essential part in looking all 'prim and proper'. So make use of these tips to make sure that you get the right haircut and enhance your look. Many who like to experiment with different hairstyles should feel gifted because your virtue of trying out new things will let you know what looks good on you and what doesn't. However there are still others who are scared to experiment. They are stuck with the same hairstyle since their teenage years. Long hair is beautiful though not always. In our busy lives if this becomes unmanageable and unruly, it is better to get a good haircut or style it accordingly. Hairstyle plays an important part in the way you look. It can make you look older if not chosen properly or younger if you adopt the right one.

Chapter Eight

Hairstyles

Take years off your face with sassy hairstyles that compliment your personality

Hairstyles for a younger look

Hair! Your crowning glory, your pride, is an essential factor that helps you in looking good. You take utmost care in caring and nourishing your coif but rarely pay attention to the way you style. Here are a few hairstyle suggestions that can make you look younger and more suave. Take years off your face with sassy hairstyles that compliment your personality.

Uber chic, updos

Classic updos, half updos, and all other variants give you a perfect young and natural look. It adds to your height and the free-flys help in framing your face making it look slimmer and younger. For half updos, take the middle portion of hair leaving aside the hair at the hairline and back of you head. Do a back comb on the middle portion and put hair spray to create a base. Now take the hair from you hair line and even it out with a comb on the middle portion. Pin it up at the back of the base. It will give you volume and puff at the crown. The loose hair can be styled in waves or curls. You can add some spark by using a few well-chosen accessories like silk flowers or other softer hair pieces.

Uber chic, updos

Loose bun

Loose buns are sexy and simple and make you look younger as they give a young belle-like appeal. They help in camouflaging older-looking skin on the neck and highlight the facial features. Gather hair into a low pony tail and fix it with a band. Divide the hair into two sections. Wrap one section of the hair in one direction till it looks like a bun. Set it up with bobby pins. Now take the second section and wrap it around the bun in the opposite direction. Again set it up with bobby pins. Don't worry if a few strands slip out as they add to the glamour quotient.

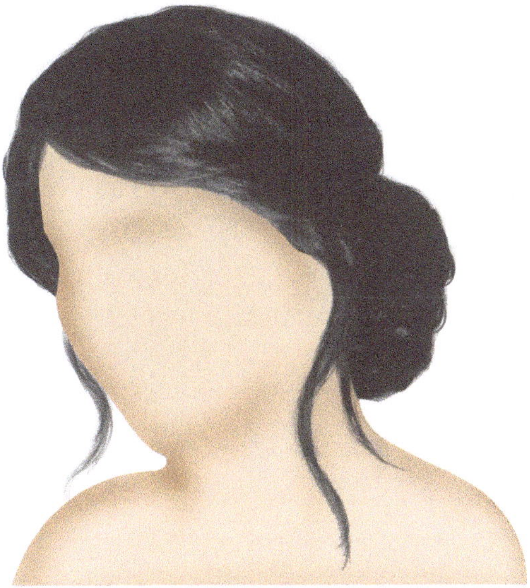

Loose bun

Curls or waves

Long, curly layers aren't meant only for teenagers. Style yourself in hot curls, loose waves for shoulder length hair, angel curls, as all of them help to shed off a few years. Soft curls look girlish and help to frame the face if you have sagging skin or contour. Make sure they're brushed through, tousled, and natural looking. You can add a few highlights to add some drama to the whole look. Apply gel or styling glaze for natural and soft curl finish that's full of bounce.

Curls or waves

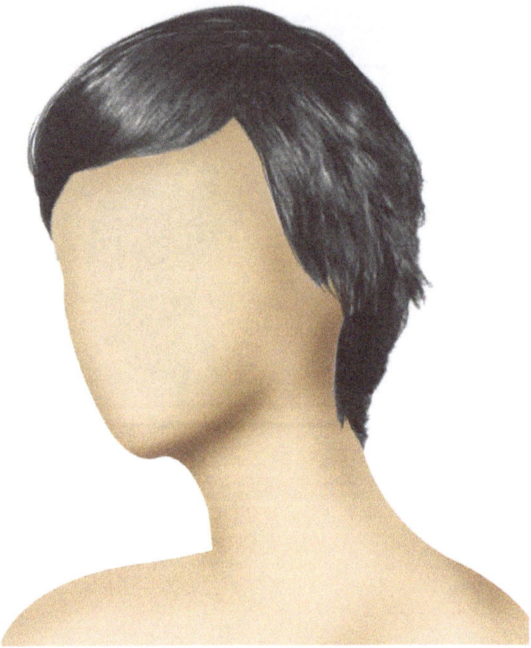

Short cuts

Short cuts

A spiky short shag or shoulder length shag helps to look younger as it lends height and volume to your hair. As we get older, hair becomes finer and this cut makes the hair look voluminous. Fine hair looks fuller when it's shorter. Add extra lift with some mousse and blow dry upside down to get volume. A side bang cut with short layers around the face and neck hides age instantly as bangs cover the fine lines on the forehead and layers cover the skin on the neck. Apply lots of lift and highlights around the face to add dimension. A tousled pixie cut with lots of layers, lots of lift, zigzag parting makes your hair look stunningly fresh as it knocks off the unnecessary volume around your jaw line giving you a slimming effect.

Chic ponytails

Ponytails are hot in all seasons and are used to create a young and glamorous look. As the hair is pulled back in a ponytail, it makes the skin on your face, especially the forehead skin look tight. Pull back your entire hair into a ponytail. Now put a band to hold the ponytail in its place. Take a small strand from the ponytail and put it around the ponytail covering the band in the process. Set it up with a bobby pin and enjoy the girlish fervour.

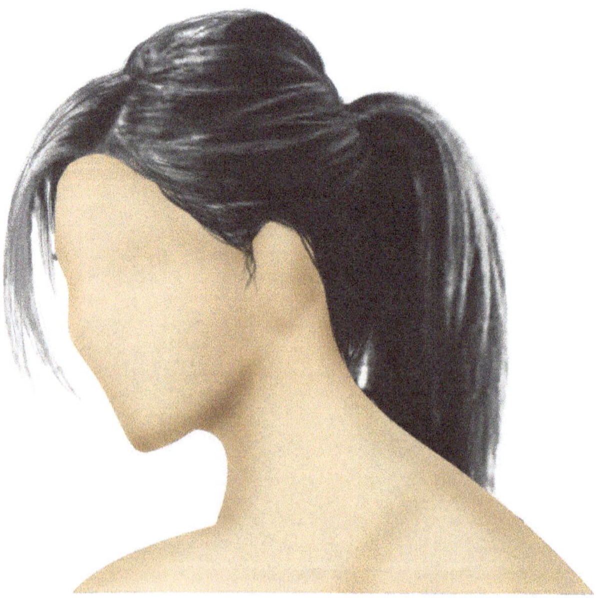

Chic ponytails

Hairstyles for weddings and parties

French roll on one side

A french roll is a classic and sophisticated hairstyle which makes a lasting impression on any wedding. It is a neat hairdo, which is done with the help of a bit of back combing and a few bobby pins. A few use French roll combs to set it to perfection. This look can be enhanced with hair brooches or hair pieces as per your dress. This style can be worn with both traditional and western wear, though it is popular mostly with western gowns or ensembles. French roll is not only for parties but is a great style for everyday wear as well.

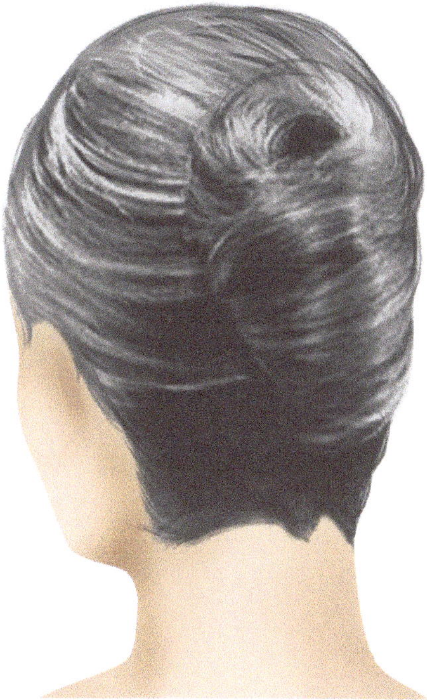

French roll on one side

Elaborate buns or plaits

Elaborate buns or plaits have been used on Indian brides since time immemorial. Each state has a specific look for their brides and these styles are modified accordingly. Not only brides, female members of both the groom's and bride's side experiment with variants in elaborate buns, plaits, and related hairstyles.

If you intend to look very traditional then these styles will enhance your overall look. This look can be accentuated with floral 'gajras', 'Tikkas', or other traditional hair pieces. This is ideal for very long hair. But those who have short hair can still manage the look with faux buns or extensions.

Elaborate buns or plaits

Elaborate updos

Elaborate updos

If you want to look like a princess or a beauty queen and add a few inches to your height, then this look is ideal for you. All elaborate updos and hairstyles start with a nice base. That base may be curls, waves, spirals, or straight hair. If you have short hair, extensions might be helpful to create the perfect look. Elaborate updos go well with modern or indo-western look. Many opt for 'Tiaras' and hair pieces with diamantes to enhance this look.

Partial updo or half updo

This is a natural-looking hairstyle for curly or long hair and is less formal. The recent trend is to wear your hairstyle down in natural curls or waves. You can add a touch of elegance by pinning part of your hair up and adding a few well-chosen accessories like silk flowers or other softer hair pieces. To give it a dramatic look, create a puff and opt for angel curls. This is good style for daytime as well as evenings. The best part is that this look can be carried in style by both teenagers as well as adults. It is simple to style and easy to manage.

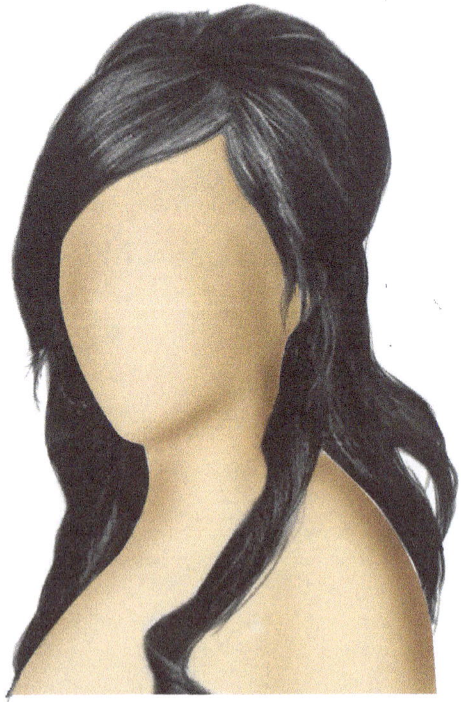

Partial updo or half updo

Loose waves or curls

Loose waves or curls are much in vogue in the wedding season. This makes up for an excellent chic look for long hair. Hair extensions can be added to achieve this effect for shorter hair. Big loose party waves or curls are easy to style and can be decorated with various head pieces including 'Tikkas'. The hair needs to be completely blow dried before setting waves or curls. This helps to add volume and create a suave look. A middle parting or a side sweep, both look good for a wedding.

Loose waves or curls

Quick Tips:

- Discuss your hairstyle well in advance with your hair stylist keeping in mind the occasion, dress, and accessories.
- Get touch-ups, colouring, streaking, extensions or any other treatment done two weeks prior to the wedding or party.
- If you have a round face, go for a side parting as this will add dimension to your face.

Choosing the right hair colour and highlights

Yes! It is very important that you choose the right hair colour and highlights. A good hair colour can make you appear bright and the wrong one can make you appear all washed out. Few women opt for golden blonde and platinum blonde colour for their hair. I need not tell you how strange they appear. I am sure you already know that. The Indian skin tone doesn't go too well with such shades. Rarely do you find someone who can carry off these shades. These are extreme cases of wrong colour application. Few of us still think of opting for subtle hair colour like honey brown highlights in huge chunks of colour throughout the hair. This looks downright tacky. Always ask for professional help. Highlighting is not something that can be done to perfection with a home kit. Choose the right colour and apply it correctly for looking great.

Here are the three things that you need to know while choosing hair colour:

- ☞ Your skin tone
- ☞ The colour of your eye
- ☞ Your natural hair colour

Your hair colour should brighten your eyes and skin tone. Avoid extreme shades. Always choose 2 to 3 shades lighter or darker than your natural hair colour.

Cool skin tone with light or brown eyes and pale hair

You can choose any shade of cool browns, ash browns, and champagne blonde, or strawberry blond colour. Don't go in for dark shades as they will make you look very pale and washed out. You will look gothic rather than beautiful.

Cool skin tone with dark eyes and dark hair

You can opt for dark browns, dark copper, and black instead of reds as you anyways reflect a lot of red and you are bound to look like a clown.

Warm skin tone with brown eyes and pale hair

You can opt for warm colours like red, copper, and light browns. These colours will enhance your skin tone.

Warm skin tone with dark eyes and dark hair

You can choose mahogany and deep reds, violet, burgundy, etc. Blue tints too can look extremely sexy on you.

Olive skin tone with brown or light eyes and pale hair

You can opt for ash browns, light browns, deep browns, copper browns, and deep reds. It will enhance your eyes.

Olive skin tone with dark eyes and dark hair

You can choose darker shades of brown and black.

Quick Tip: Red is the most difficult hair colour to maintain. So, if you want maintenance-free hair colour, you may want to avoid red. Those who are interested in using red hair colour should choose coppery reds instead of the bluish reds. Coppery undertones provide a more natural looking finish to your hair.

Hair extensions

Not every woman on earth is blessed with long and voluminous hair. It's also a fact that not all stars have long locks of flowing hair. The answer to your hair woes at times lies in hair extensions. Hair extensions are sometimes made up of synthetic fibres like nylon or other non-flammable material and most of the times with human hair. They add the required volume and length to your hair. There are many types of hair extensions like front bang extensions, single strand extensions in various colours to be used as highlights as well, half wig-like extensions to be placed behind your head or from the crown area to add more volume. But we will discuss the extensions in general terms discussing only the most common ones used.

Single strand extensions

Single strand extensions are nothing but a single lock of hair that can be clamped, glued, or melted with your original hair. You also get clip in single strands so that you can fix them when required and take them off before going to sleep. Single strand extensions are applied to your hair strands a bit away from the scalp, so when you style it or leave your hair loose, the natural hair covers them up perfectly and they are not visible easily. Single strand extensions come in various shades and colours. At times they come in crazy neon colours to be used when going for a party. The individual method involves taking small amounts (around 20-50 strands) of extension hair (natural or synthetic) and applying to small sections of your own hair by either weaving-in, heat fusing, gluing, clamping, binding them with rings, or using waxes and protein polymers. All of these methods involve coating your own hair with a chemical or foreign substance. These extensions last for a few months before they have to be taken out and completely re-done. The main problem with this method is taking the hair extensions out without damaging your own hair.

Single strand hair extension

Clip-in hair weft extensions

A weft looks like a little curtain of hair attached together at the top and free flowing hair at the bottom. Wefts can be made by machine, but the best wefts are the ones that are handmade. Handmade wefts are custom made to suit your head perfectly. Handmade wefts tend to last much longer and are generally thicker than machine-made ones. These come in clip-in versions as well as can be weaved into your hair with tiny braids. Let us discuss the clip in version which is more popular these days. The thread-like structure which binds the locks of hair into a weft has clips. Whenever you need to add some volume and length to your hair, clip-in weft of hair at regular intervals below your crown area and move downwards. Wefts are applied horizontally on your head in layers. As the hair of the crown area falls on these extensions, they become invisible. Though, you can't style them much, you can use them if you need to add length and volume to your existing hairstyle which is very helpful. Remove them before going off to sleep. You can actually wear these hair extensions all day long. They do less damage to your hair in comparison to glued extensions.

Clip-in hair weft extension

½ head wig extensions

As the name suggests, these are like half-head wigs which can be clipped into your own natural hair around the crown area and the neck. This is crafted like a wig so you will immediately have a voluminous length of hair at your disposal. This can be styled as well. Just make sure that they are properly clipped-in into your head to match your natural hair. The hair at the crown area covers the clip-ons and makes them invisible to the onlooker.

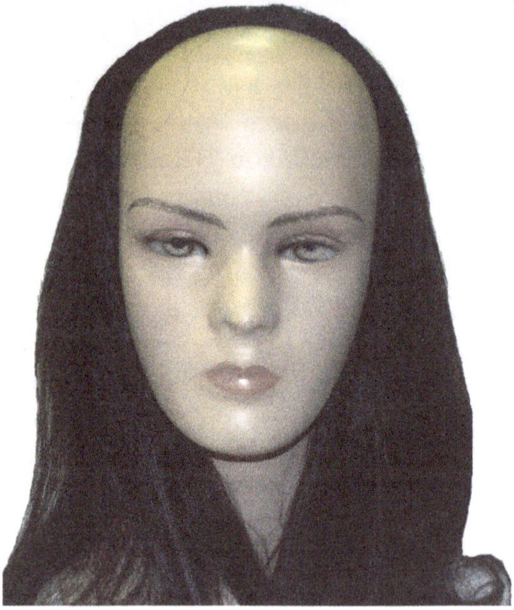

½ head wig extension

¾th head wig extensions

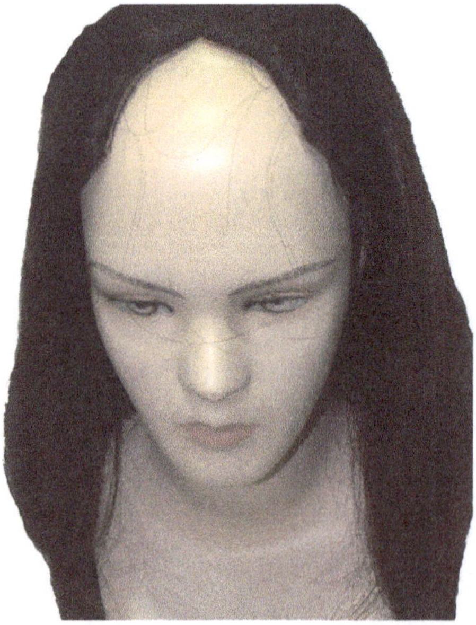

¾th head wig extension

This resembles a proper wig except that it covers the area around the head and not the top (think of the letter 'V' while imagining the kind of coverage this gives. You comb out hair near the partition and clip-in the extension around the head. Then let the natural hair around the partition area fall on the extension for a more natural look. The natural hair will cover the clip-ons and make them invisible. This can be styled in any way you like. Just make sure that they are properly clipped-in into your head and match your natural hair.

Buns and rolls

This is the most popular hair extension since time immemorial. We have seen our mothers use it whenever they wanted to attend a wedding or a party. We have also used it at one point or the other (especially as many of us do not have very long hair). But the quality of such hair extensions has increased manifolds today. These come in a pre-shaped form of a bun or a roll. You will get various designs and variations and they are gently fixed into our own hair with the help of hair pins.

Buns and rolls

After care

You need to look after your Hair Extensions in much the same way as you would look after your own hair. Here are a few tips:

- ☞ Wash condition and moisturise your hair every 2-3 days. The extensions do not receive your natural scalp oils so need to have moisture added with every wash. If you don't moisturise your hair extensions they will become brittle and break easily leading to split ends. Apply a good moisturiser for Hair Extensions.
- ☞ Treat them carefully. Do not yank them with a brush, burn them with heating equipments (blow dryer, straighteners), or destroy them with chemicals (hair colour etc).
- ☞ Always brush out all knots before you wash your hair, swim, or sleep. Start at the bottom and work your way up slowly using a paddle brush.
- ☞ Make sure you wash in between the weaves to keep your scalp clean and free of bacteria.
- ☞ Every 6-8 weeks your own hair would have grown about 1 to 1 1/2 inches. The weaving will still be intact and the strands will still be attached to the natural hair. At this time you will need to return to your extensions artist and have the procedure redone. The expert will check for any product build up, damage etc. You can have any length of extensions applied to your hair. You can have about 26 inch-30 inch long extensions applied to your hair as well. Any natural hair over this length is about 8 - 10 years old at the ends and it loses its quality. Also, anything longer than this, puts extra weight on your scalp which may lead to uneven pressure and damage to your own hair and its roots. The best looking hair extensions for average height women are usually around 22 inches or less. The most popular length is 18 inch which is hangs until your bra line.

Quick Tip: Use clip-on hair extensions. Though a bit cumbersome to apply everyday but they will make you look sexy with great looking hair and cause less damage than conventional hair weaving.

Chapter Nine

Hair care

Your hair is like a health barometer which shows the actual condition of your health in general

Hair care

Your crowning glory is your pride. If your mane is manageable, then you are amongst the lucky few who are blessed with such a beautiful gift. A sense of beauty and well being is reflected by a person who has healthy hair. Your precious mane accentuates your looks and balances your attire. Investment in good hair products which promote healthy hair goes a long way.

Most of us face stress in one way or the other because of the messed up condition of our tresses.

There are so many problems which cause a concern like greying, breakage, dandruff but the most common problem is hair fall.

Hair fall and oiling; does it help?

A normal cycle of hair growth lasts for 2-6 years. In a month, each hair grows approximately one centimetre during this phase of growth. About 90 percent of the hair on your scalp grows at any one time. And the other 10 percent of the hair on your scalp is in a resting phase. After 2 to 3 months, the resting hair falls out and new hair starts to grow in its place. It is normal to shed some hair each day as part of this cycle.

Hair fall and oil

Your hair is like a health barometer which shows the actual condition of your health in general. Your hair can be affected by diet, illness, medication and environmental factors. A lot of people face hair fall but not many go to a trichologist to get a remedy. Instead, they go for remedies that are available in their household, or get the best alternative available in the market. Many hair oil brands claim to cure hair fall and help in re-growth. Herbs like Jojoba and others are listed as the magic potions which claim to help in hair growth. And as gullible customers you tend to try out the product at least once.

But the question arises that 'Does hair oil really help in hair growth?' Grandma remedies list hot coconut oil massage once a week for beautifying, strengthening and growth of hair. Many of us follow this regimen strictly.

The market is flooded with several brands of herbal oils, medicinal oils that promise hair growth, as people are ready to try natural oils like Mustard, Almond, Coconut and even Castor oil to have better growth or re-growth of hair. It is also a fact though that there is no known proof of its effectiveness.

Hair experts suggest oiling to be a healthy practice; an advice that has been followed through several years. Traditionally, coconut oil massage helps the hair shaft look nourished and conditioned. But it is a myth to think that it penetrates through the hair to promote growth. Oil is good if left for an hour or two or maximum overnight. The application of oil on the hair is good if done once a week. But most importantly, what is equally important is that the oil should be thoroughly taken off your hair. Many experts suggest that oil acts as a medium to get nourishment to the roots. Oil massage activates blood cells on the scalp which eventually gives rise to hair growth. So it's not the oil that promotes growth, it's the massage that circulates blood and oxygen to the roots and helps in promoting growth.

Should you feel that your coiffure concerns are not completely met by oiling your hair religiously; then you should opt for extra care, a good diet and treatment to have a healthy mane. Hair oil provides the conditioning and nourishment required for a healthy look.

Is hair-wash a must daily?

Everybody wants their hair to look clean and beautiful. Should you wash your hair daily is a question which many want to decipher. Many believe that regular washing of hair leads to dryness and hair fall.

Hair experts suggest that washing hair daily is subjective. Frequency of washes every week is based on the climate, the job, and condition of your hair.

Keeping the hair and scalp clean is a must. Anybody who has a sweaty and oily scalp should wash hair more frequently. Use a mild shampoo and condition the end of the hair to avoid dryness.

If your hair is excessively frizzy or dry avoid washing it daily. But if you have an oily and sweaty scalp then you need to wash your hair daily.

Diluting the shampoo helps in avoiding dryness. Avoid applying shampoos with conditioner as conditioner on scalp is not good for hair. Good products if applied as per your hair type or condition can never lead to dryness or breakage.

Does hair colour cause damage in the long run?

Many want to experiment with their looks and go for global colouring or highlights. But the question arises if hair colour damages hair in the long run?

There are three types of hair colour: permanent, semi-permanent and temporary. All have chemicals in varying levels. Permanent dyes are harsher than the other variants. The dye mixture makes the hair shaft swell to accept the colour.

Our hair has a form of protein known as keratin and the sulphur in the dye oxidizes with the chemicals and hair protein to allow colour change.

Hair colour

Hair experts' comments

- ☞ Hair colouring, if not done properly may cause damage. Colouring opens up the cuticles on the hair shaft and dries up the cortex (second layer of hair) making it brittle and easily breakable.
- ☞ Over use of dyes, dyes left to develop for more than the required time and other form of abuse can damage hair. Aftercare with proper products is necessary to maintain the health of the hair.
- ☞ Protect hair with colour specific products to prevent dryness or dulling in the long run. There are many mild shampoos or conditioners for coloured hair. The ones which are 'sulphate' free react less with your hair and colour.

How to prepare hair for a special occasion?

Here's a hair care guide for perfectly lustrous, healthy hair in time for any special occasion:

Firstly visit your hair stylist at least three months before the pre-planned occasion like wedding, to set up a hair care regimen. This will help you to get a perfect, glossy and healthy mane.

Hair experts suggest that women should take hot oil treatment and Hair spas once in a week (for a month) to ensure that their hair retains moisture and is conditioned from deep within. This will make their hair strong to bear all the styling on the D day. Keratin hair treatment two weeks prior to the party or wedding also helps to have frizz free, smooth and shiny hair.

For brides it is very important to settle on a hairstyle before they choose a headpiece or a veil as per the dress, make-up and occasion. It is important to be absolutely confident about the final look for the wedding. Practice the look prior to the wedding by setting up a rehearsal with your stylist. If you are planning touch-ups, extensions, a haircut, trim or any other treatment, get it done well in advance. Touch-ups should be done two weeks prior to the party or wedding day to create a perfect base. Hair-extensions help in adding volume and texture to your hair, therefore, discuss all these aspects (like length, colour, streaks, etc.) with your stylist bearing in mind the hairstyle on the D day.

Excercise

Save your hair from extreme temperatures. Try to avoid strong winds which will entangle your hair or long sun exposure which will make them dry and brittle. Make sure to cover your hair with a scarf or cap before you step out.

Use wide toothed comb on your precious mane to gently detangle lest your hair breaks or splits. Apply good quality products on your hair and avoid blow drying, straightening or crimping unnecessarily.

Ensure a good diet full of protein for a naturally healthy hair. Hair grows and sheds in every three months, so make sure you avoid junk and spicy food well in advance. Drinking at least 8 glasses of water in a day and increasing the consumption of fresh fruits and vegetables will help improve the overall health of your hair.

Have at least 8 hours of sleep and engage in aerobics or other cardiovascular exercise that help proper blood circulation. Avoid stress as much as possible as stress leads to hair fall and other problems. Good health and complete rest are key to lustrous hair.

Is hair spa beneficial?

With prolonged lack of hair care in addition to regular wear and tear, your hair loses its vitality and shine over a period of time. Moreover, stress and other damaging factors force your hair to bear problems like, hair loss, split ends, dandruff, dull and lifeless hair, oily scalp, etc. In this case many experts recommend regular hair spa to revive the lost beauty. A hair spa involves oil massage, followed by shampoo and deep conditioning treatment.

The oil massage helps to improve blood circulation to the roots and helps in hair growth. Shampoo cleans up every spec of unwanted oil on the hair and scalp making it grime and dirt free.

Hair Spa

After this, a deep conditioning pack is applied to the hair followed by a session with a hair steamer so that the conditioner goes deep into the hair follicles, making it soft and shiny.

Hair Experts say

- Hair spa is a must once a month to lock in the moisture in dry winter months as well as in hot months. These are the times when your hair loses excess moisture due to harsh weather.
- A hair spa helps in combating frizz as it deeply conditions and nourishes hair.
- It also helps in relieving stress as the massage to the roots of the hair and on the pressure points soothes the nerves.
- Hair spa can be done at a salon or at home with a home kit. You need to apply a hair treatment mask, cover it with a shower cap and keep it on for a specified period and then rinse thoroughly with warm water for best results.
- If you massage your hair with coconut oil before hand, it will add more sheen to your hair. But make sure to use quality products.
- Hair spas also deeply hydrate and nourishes, making your hair look naturally beautiful and shiny. It helps to reduce frizz and curls and adds bounce and volume to your hair.
- It helps to decrease the damage done by pollution and extreme weather conditions.

Taking care of hair in extremely hot weather

Summer months bring in heat, dust and sweat. Exposure to sun and heat can cause your hair to become dry, brittle and frizzy. Similarly extremely dry and cold months can have the same effect on your hair.

Your hair should be kept clean and nourished to avoid any problems. Hair experts state that, if your scalp is sweaty and oily then wash your hair daily with a mild shampoo. Avoid applying shampoo with conditioner as it is not a good idea to apply conditioner to your scalp. Instead apply a good conditioner to your hair ends, to keep it nourished and to avoid frizz.

Do not overdo heat treatment

Summer means dryness. Try and avoid usage of styling and curling equipments on your hair like tongs, straigtheners, blow dryers etc., during the summer months. Your hair is prone to breakage and dryness if you cause more heat damage with the use of these equipments. Instead let them dry naturally and keep them conditioned at all times. You should ideally pamper your hair with a hair-spa at least once a month to lock in the moisture.

Avoid using a lot of styling products on your hair like gels, mousse, sprays, etc. The summer heat will anyways make your hair sticky and dirty and if you use these products they often attract more dirt and grime, further causing hair problems.

Summer means frequent visits to beaches and pool sides. Harsh sun rays can play havoc with your tresses and so can the salt (in sea water) and chlorine (in pool water). Not only your hair is affected, even your scalp can become sensitive and itchy because of these factors.

The way your skin requires protection from the sun and other damaging factors with the help of sunscreen, in much the same way does the hair require a protective cover. Oiling your hair before going for a dip or applying generous amount of leave-in conditioner to your hair helps counterfeit the damaging effect of the sun rays and the chemicals, like chlorine in the water. Follow up a dip with a quick hair wash, to remove any traces of chemicals and oil from hair. A hat or an umbrella also comes handy when you are stepping out in the sun to avoid direct exposure to sun rays.

Summer means dehydration. This also affects your hair and can cause hair fall due to dryness. Try to drink 2-3 litres of water every day. Carbonated drinks, tea and coffee make you dehydrated, therefore choose from herbal tea, fresh fruit juices and flavoured water to quench your thirst. Your hair will shine with vitality if you are not dehydrated.

Taking care of hair in wet and damp weather

Monsoons are not the ideal season to get any chemical treatments done. Unruly locks, frizzy hair are a regular complaint in the wet season. You might get drenched and feel wet, but the season doesn't add moisture to your precious mane.

The heightened moisture makes your hair flat and its texture dull, plus the problems like stickiness, greasiness and dandruff arise. There's nothing to fret though as with proper care you can still have gorgeous looking hair each monsoon. Let's find out about the many no-no's to follow up in monsoons and have healthy and beautiful hair.

Don't go for colouring or any other chemical treatments during monsoons. Hair is prone to dryness and the scalp is very sensitive during this season, making it prone to allergies and rashes. Moreover, chlorine and salt in water is comparatively higher this season and hard on colour and chemically treated hair.

Avoid getting your hair wet in the rains. Rainwater brings down pollutants in the air; these pollutants damage the hair and make it look dull and limp.

Do not comb your hair when they are wet as they are prone to breakage. Don't use straightening irons directly either. Straightening irons make your hair shaft weak resulting in a lot of breakage.

Do not over-shampoo your hair as it tends to become frizzy. Combat regular stickiness and grime by using a mild shampoo. You can use the shampoo either every day or every other day as need be. However bear in mind to use a good quality shampoo and conditioner for maintaining your glossy mane.

By all means do not apply the conditioner on the scalp. Scalp application doesn't help in getting rid of the itchiness and dandruff which occurs during this season. Instead apply the conditioner on the hair ends to tame frizz and get smooth hair.

Don't use hair sprays and styling gels or other hair products until it is absolutely necessary, as the lacquers and gums in these products stick to the scalp and cause dandruff in this season.

Don't leave oil in your hair for over an hour. Oil massage may help your hair look shiny and healthy but it may cause dandruff if left for long as it attracts dirt and grime. Keep your hair clean for optimum health.

Minimise the use of hot tongs and curling irons. The hair is anyway traumatised with the wet weather, stickiness and grease. If a lot of heating appliances are used it might even become dry and frizzier and eventually break.

Do not tie your hair into a pony or a bun when wet. This can damage the roots and cause breakage. Let the hair dry naturally.

Taking care of hair in extremely cold weather

Extreme cold and dryness can also cause dry, frizzy, and lifeless hair. Winter months are too cold and the moisture content is less. This affects the condition of your hair and makes them susceptible to break easily.

Oil your hair and opt for deep conditioning treatments. Do not let it sit overnight on your scalp lest you catch cold. A steam treatment along with deep conditioning will help the moisture content to penetrate deep into the hair shaft.

Minimise the use of hot tongs and curling irons. This will increase the brittleness of the hair and your hair might face breakage.

Avoid washing your hair in excessively hot water. Hot water will wash off the natural oils completely and damage your hair. Rinse in tepid/cold water for smooth and shiny hair.

Try not to leave your hair loose when you go out. Either cover them up or tie them into a good style. This will help lock in moisture the most and prevent the dry winter hair to make it frizzy and dull.

Go in for regular trims to avoid split ends. Use leave-in conditioners to keep hair ends moisturised. It is as good as cold cream protecting your skin in the winter months.

It is normal for 20-50 hair strands to break each day. But if you see abnormal breakage or loss of a huge lock of hair, consult a hair expert or trichologist immediately. Eat food rich in iron and protein for naturally healthy growth of hair. Protein is found in meat, fish, poultry, milk, eggs, cheese, and yogurt. And Iron can be obtained by consuming spinach, cockles, liver, kidneys, pulses, lentils, beans, peas, and dried fruits.

If you abuse your hair less, they will remain loyal to you for a longer period of time in full glory. Proper hair care will ensure that you can enjoy your beauty for long.

Chapter Ten

Make-up according to the face cut and make-up tricks

Make-up makes up for most of your drawbacks

Make-up can make or break your look. It covers uneven skin tone, marks and blemishes, under eye dark circles and many other problem areas. Make-up helps in making you look different instantly.

You need not go under the knife to improve your looks. Make-up, if applied correctly, can give you a youthful and glamorous look.

Incorrect make-up can transform you into a cakey devil. So be very careful while applying. A handful of women actually pay attention to applying make-up as per the face type. Not many know how to accentuate their best feature. Make-up should be applied according to your facial features and face shape to make you look graceful instead of made up. Let us quickly remember the basic face shapes which will help us to chalk out the make-up plan for each face shape. The basic six shapes are Oval, Heart, Triangle, Square, Round, and Rectangle or Oblong.

Make-up kit

Oval

Oval is the perfectly symmetrical face shape. The most balanced face shape, the sides of such a face are flat, with a wide forehead; one that is high, with a square chin. If you possess this shape, you are truly blessed.

As everything is in symmetry, light make-up suits the oval face shape the best. Choose light-coloured blushes, shadows, and lipstick. The aim is to look as natural as possible.

Foundation: First, apply a darker shade of foundation, followed by a lighter one. Apply the darker shade on the temples. Shade the face with both light and dark foundation. Apply light foundation in the middle portion of the face for that balanced look. Apply translucent powder on the lighter foundation parts like the eyes, cheekbones, nose, and forehead.

Concealer: A cream concealer can be used to cover blemishes and marks. Apply with a sponge, making sure to cover the area from under the eyes to the cheekbones. Using a concealer in the center of the forehead is a good idea.

Blush: Apply a light blush just to highlight the apple of your cheeks to give it a rounder effect.

Eye make-up: Instead of using eyeliner, use a brown eye pencil.

Lipstick: Finally apply the light or natural-coloured lipstick.

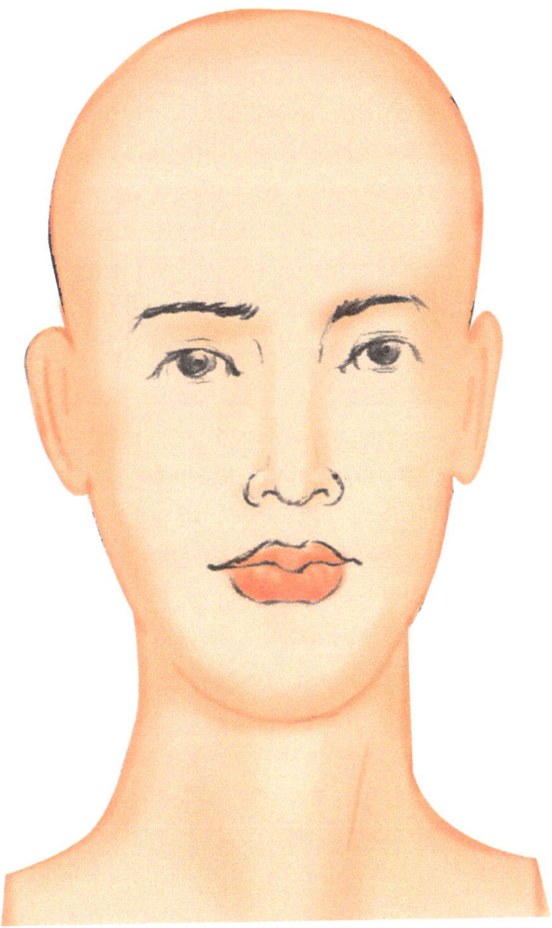

Oval shape

Heart

This is a shape that is wider at the forehead and narrow towards the chin. A heart-shaped face should have the blusher used on the cheekbones and not on the apples. The blusher should be blended carefully. Any application of colour should be avoided in the middle of the face. If this is done, it will result in a balancing effect. Using darker contour shades will help in giving it that receding look for any protruding bone structure.

Foundation: The heart-shaped face is wide on the forehead, so use a darker contour around the forehead. You want to reduce the temple area by the use of a darker contour in giving it an oval appearance. The heart-shaped face is wide in the cheek area, and to reduce it, you should apply dark foundation to the cheek area nearest to the hairline. This will make the cheeks look slimmer. With the help of your cosmetic sponge, blend in the darker contour to the hairline.

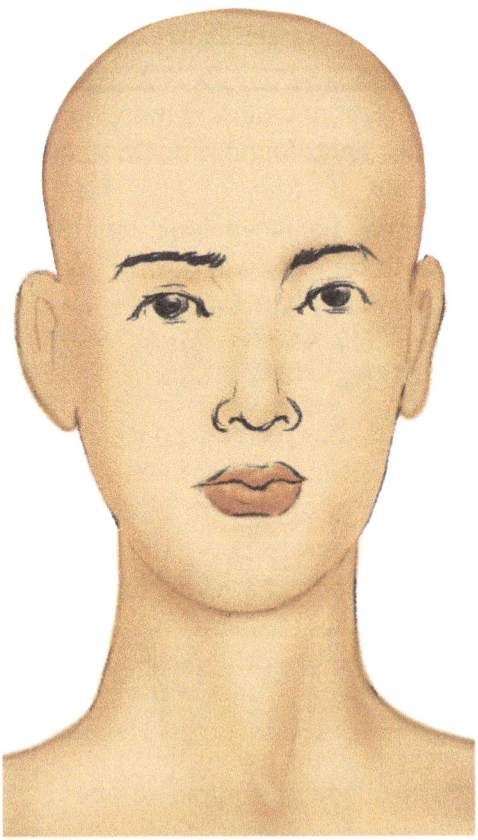

Heart shape

Concealer: Apply with a sponge, making sure to cover the area from under the eyes to the cheekbones. The area around your nose and mouth should also be dealt with effective coverage.

Blush: To bring out the best in a heart-shaped face, highlight the cheekbones with white. Put blusher beneath this and on the chin. Apply blush with an angular movement and not a vertical movement while creating a contour.

Eye make-up: Highlight your eyes with light make-up. A lighter eye-shadow will open up your eyes and draw attention to them. Apply thin eyeliner and kajal.

Lipstick: Highlight your lips with a lipstick that suits your skin tone.

Triangle

Your face has a narrow forehead that flares to a wide chin. The aim is to balance your forehead with the chin to make it as close as possible to an oval shape.

Foundation: To balance the shape of the face, apply a shade of the foundation that is a tone darker than your complexion around the jaw line. This will make your face look slimmer around your jaw. Apply the foundation, a shade lighter than your skin tone, on your forehead and nose area. This will make it look broader.

Concealer: Apply with a sponge, making sure to cover the area from under the eyes to the cheekbones as well as area around your nose and chin.

Blush: Highlight the middle of your face with a good blush. Sweep it across the apple of the cheeks towards your cheekbones.

Eye make-up: Highlight your eyes with dark make-up or subtle smokey eyes during daytime and make them look bigger. Highlight your eyebrows with a defined shape. This will shift the focus on your features rather than the shape of your face.

Lipstick: Keep your lips subtle with a good gloss and lipstick. Do not use harsh lip liner. The idea is to balance the face, yet bring less focus to your jaw area. Play up with pastel colours. Avoid muted and dark colours.

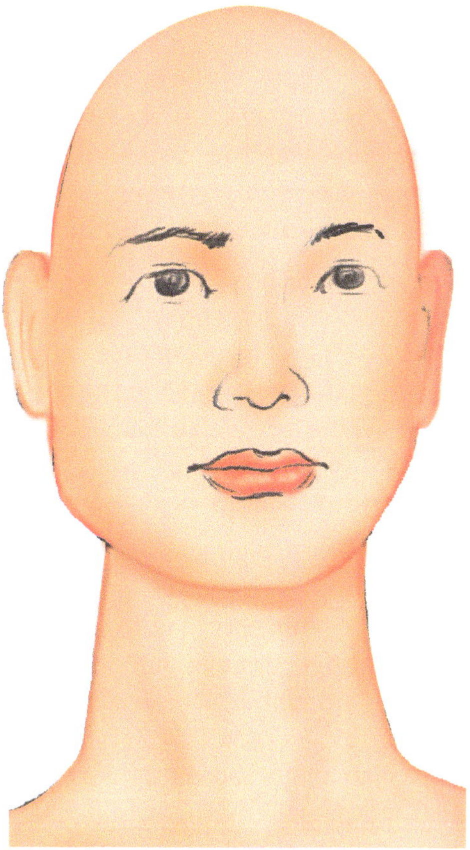

Triangle shape

Square

A square face has a very pronounced jaw line. It is wider around the jaw and chin. And the aim should be to make it look slim around the jaw area.

Foundation: To balance the face shape, apply foundation which is one tone darker than your complexion. This will make your face look slimmer. Apply it right through the cheekbone to the jaw area, slimming out the pronounced jaw line.

Concealer: Apply with a sponge, making sure to cover the area from under the eyes to the cheekbones. Also, apply it on the corners of your nose and area around the chin.

Blush: Apply blusher from the apple of the cheeks and sweep it across the cheekbones. Soften a square face with shading from the jaw line to the cheeks. Then narrow the face with colour above the temples. Blend your blush well. Do not create deep contours.

Eye make-up: To highlight your eyes, use both the eyeliner and the eye pencil. Define your eyes to make them look bigger. Use softer eye shadow and highlight the beautiful shape of your eyes. Do not use edgy eye shadow styles which might accentuate your angular features. Remember to blend your eye shadows well.

Lipstick: Apply a lipstick which suits your skin tone and goes well with your dress. Use a nude pencil on the lip line and fill up the lips with glossy colour. The idea is to create a pouty and glossy look to soften your angular features.

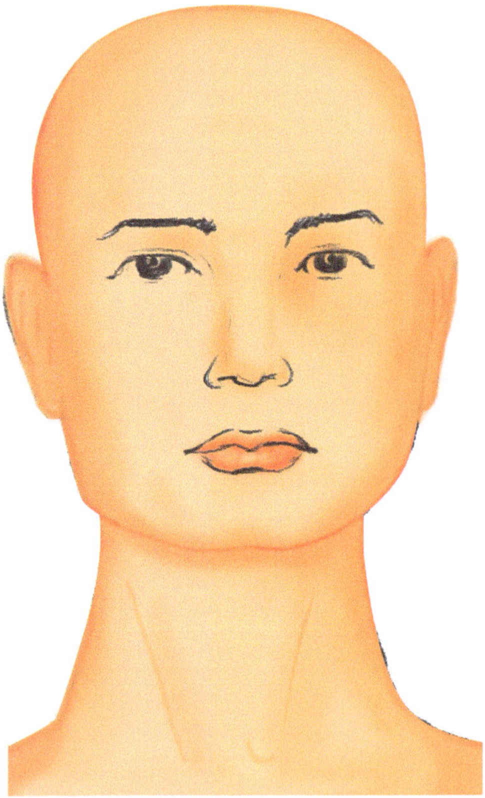

Square shape

Round

The aim is to give dimension to a round face and reduce its roundness. Your cheeks are full, your face is a symmetrical and uniform size, with no jutting or angular features. It is a chubby face.

Foundation: Apply foundation matching your skin tone. Apply a darker shade foundation around your cheeks to make your face look slim and reduce the plumpness. You can also apply a light foundation shade over the centre of your nose to narrow.

Concealer: Blend the concealer with a sponge under the eyes, the sides of the nose and out to the upper cheeks. Make a round face slimmer by shading the jaw line, the cheeks, and above the brow bone. Also, highlight the sides and tip of the nose.

Blush: After you have re-shaped your face, apply powder and blusher. Apply blusher by using your nose as a guide. Apply blush on your cheekbones, creating a sculpted look around your cheeks. Sweep the blush from the apple of the cheeks to the end of cheekbone ending near your ears. Use highlighter under your brows and on your cheekbones.

Eye make-up: Make your eyes dark with kohl or kajal. You can also apply thick eyeliner to highlight your eyes. Opt for the smokey-eye effect.

Lipstick: Keep your lips natural or just use gloss. As this face does not have any dominant features, you have to accentuate features to highlight the parts to make it elongated. Concentrate on the areas from the lower lip to the chin downwards and from the eyebrows to the hairline.

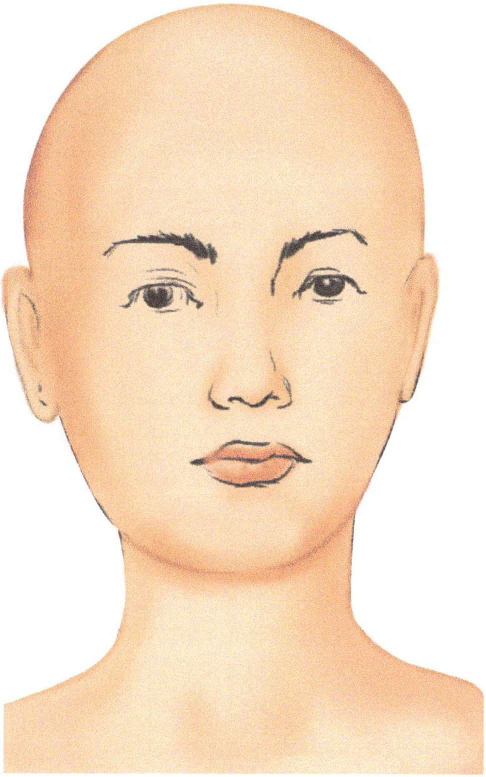

Round shape

Rectangle or oblong

On the whole, your features are long and angular. Most of the length from the eye to the chin area is long. The long face has high cheekbones, a broad forehead, and a strong sharp chiselled jaw line. If you have a long face, the last thing you should do is highlight or contour your face as this will make you face appear even longer. Brushing a bit of bronzer across your chin will give it an impression of a shorter chin. The idea is to reduce the long shape of your face and balance it with good make-up.

Foundation: Use a foundation that is a shade lighter than your skin tone on the forehead and neckline and foundation matching your skin tone on the rest of the face.

Concealer: Apply with a sponge, making sure to cover the area from under the eyes to the cheekbones.

Blush: Apply very light blush just on the apple of your cheeks. Do not over do blush at any cost. To give the face a shortened look, apply blusher on the cheekbones and blend it towards the apples of the cheeks. By applying a highlighter to the chin, you can also get that shortening effect. When you apply your blush, you should start closer in on the apples of your cheeks and brush in a outward motion across the face, mostly upwards.

Eye make-up: Apply thin eyeliner or just line the tear line of your eye with kajal.

Lipstick: Outline your lips with a lip liner and put lipstick evenly with the help of a lip brush.

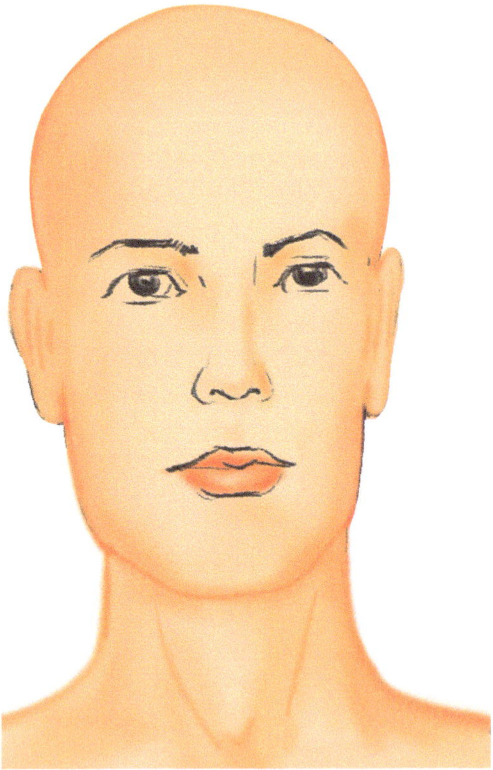

Rectangle shape

Quick Tip: A right shade of red gives a woman the ultimate feminine look and a touch of elegance. But how can you choose a perfect red lipstick for yourself? Ascertain your skin tone to choose the right lipstick for you. Categorise your skin tone under cool, warm, or neutral. If the skin reflects red or orange undertones, your skin tone is warm. If it's peach, yellow or olive, your skin tone is neutral. Blue and pink undertones mean your skin tone is cool. If you are warm toned then look for a lipstick which has brick, copper, wine, and coral red undertones. If you have a neutral skin tone, look for orange or brown undertones. If your skin colour reflects cool tones then go for ruby, garnet shades of berry and fuchsia red undertones. If your complexion is on the paler side, try to use softer pigments unless you want to give yourself a gothic and a dramatic look. Similarly, choose other shades of lipstick keeping in mind your skin tone.

Make-up tricks

Your eyes are the window to your soul. And you want them to look big, bright and beautiful all the time. Here's how you can accentuate your eyes in all shapes and sizes with perfection.

Make-up for different eye shapes

1. Big bulging eyes: If you have big, bulging and round eyes the aim should be to elongate them. Apply medium to dark eye-shadow on the eyelid up to the crease. Extend the eye-shadow to the outer corner and continue down along the lower lid. Use black liner to line top and bottom lid to make your eyes appear smaller. Apply mascara on the upper lashes towards the outer half.

2. Small eyes: If you want to create the effect of big, beautiful eyes, choose light eye-shadow. To make your eyes look bigger, use the creamy white eyeliner pencil in the bottom eyelids. Never line the inner edge of the lower eyelashes; this would make your eyes look smaller. Black eyeliner makes the eyes appear smaller. Go for

Eye shapes

brown or navy instead. Curl your eyelashes; it will open up your eyes. Finish your eye make-up with a layer of volume- adding mascara. Slightly arched brows can help to make your eyes look bigger.

3. Deep set eyes: If you have deep set eyes, choose light eye-shadow, it would help to make your eyes appear bigger. Apply light eye-shadows on your eyelid from the inner corner of your eye to the outer. Light colours should be applied in the middle of the lid, and darker colours on and just above the socket line. Blend the shades out.

4. Wide set eyes: You can visually reduce the range between your eyes if you apply a dark eye-shadow from the outer corner of your eye to the middle of the eyelid. Apply a light eye-shadow from the middle of your eyelid to the inner corner of your eye. Blend in different shades in the middle of the eyelid.

5. Close set eyes: Apply some concealer on the inner corners of both eyes. Using an eyeliner; draw a very thin line along the upper eyelashes and make it thicker near the outer corner of your eyes. Apply a very thin layer of light eye-shadow from the inner corner of your eyes to the middle of your eyelid. Then apply dark eye-shadow starting from the middle of your eyelid to the outer corner. Blend the colours in the middle of the eyelids. Use more mascara on the outer corners. This will widen the distance between your eyes.

6. Down turned eyes: Apply eye-shadow outwards and upwards. Apply eyeliner close to the upper lash line and then blend in the shadow along the socket line in the outer two- thirds of the eyes. Apply volumising mascara to open up the eyes. This will give an upturned effect.

7. Hooded eyes: If you have hooded eyes, apply light eye-shadow on your eyelids. Use a pencil to make a thick smoky line along the upper eyelashes to make the eyes appear less hooded. Make sure that the line is thick enough to be seen when your eyes are open. Under the lower eyelashes, draw a thin liner. Apply volumising mascara to open up the eyes. You just don't have to apply eyeliner and call it a day. Try these different make-up tricks to enhance your peepers.

How to make your nose look slimmer?

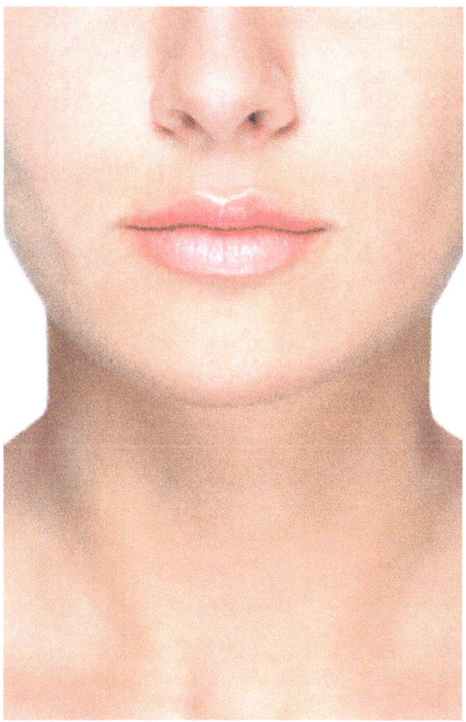

Not all your features are perfect. And if the nose appears flattened and wide, it just feels awful at the time you are getting all decked up and glam. Many of us curse our stars that why we didn't get a sharp nose and instead got an inflated bump in the middle of our face. Worry not ladies. There are ways to deal with a wide nose. You can make it appear slimmer with the help of simple make-up techniques.

For a wide nose draw a contour with darker colour shade. Darker lines should be straight at the sides, and not too thick. Blend them well. These lines must start from eyebrows and finish at the end of the tip.

To better render the impression of a thin nose, draw a straight bright line at the middle of the nose and blend it well.

How: Apply a concealer on the bridge of the nose and then put some powder, about two shades lighter than your skin tone on top of your nose. There are correctors or concealer palettes available in the market with both lighter and darker shades which can be used for this purpose. Brands like RCMA Sampler Foundation Palette will suit everyone's needs.

Use an eye-shadow that is a little darker than your skin, and put it on the sides of your nose to make it look thinner. You can also use a brown lip pencil instead, and draw two lines on either side of the nose and blend it well to create the same illusion. There are corrector pens available as well like MAC NW45 corrector stick can help you draw and blend lines in the same manner. Draw a straight line down the side of your nose from the inner corner of your eye starting from your brow to the ball of your nose at the tip. Brush the sides of the nose with powder, two shades darker than your skin tone, to get the perfect slimming effect.

Make sure that the foundation powder and the concealer you use is matte, making your nose appear less shiny and less attention will be drawn to it.

Another way to draw attention away from your nose is to apply more make-up to your eyes.

How to make your lips fuller?

Luscious, full, and plump lips are most women's dream. Everybody wants an Angelina Jolie pout. How can you get that result without painful cosmetic surgery and injections? Use make-up to make your lips look fuller!

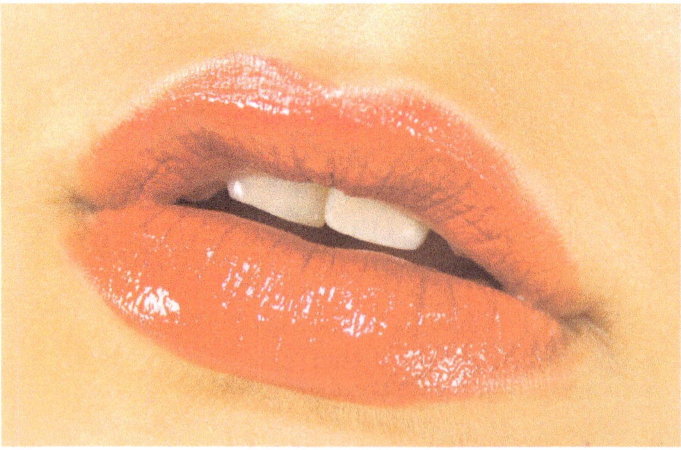

Cover your lips with foundation or concealer and blend well. Select a lip liner close to the natural lip colour for realistic results. Use it to line the lips just outside of the lip line, starting in the middle of the top lip and working towards each corner.

Stay close to the natural lip line to keep a realistic appearance.

Check for balance on each side and see if the line drawn by you looks even. This will help keep a natural look. Use the same liner to completely fill colour in the lips. Be sure that there are no obvious lines. Blot the liner with tissue if necessary or blend with a finger.

Finish the look with a clear or natural-coloured gloss. Apply the gloss all over the lips that will give the illusion of fullness.

Also, lip plumping products are available in the market. They have natural ingredients like cinnamon which tingle and activate the skin cells on the lips, giving them a fuller and plumped look. The market is flooded with a range of products like Avon Plump pout lip gloss or MaxoLip.

What is air-brush make-up?

Models on magazine covers look 10 on 10 perfect, thanks to softwares like Photoshop. It can turn a beast into beauty and vice-versa. But models on the ramp who display a flawless skin tone or tan, are they real? Few are gifted with beautiful and clear skin, but most of them use good make-up techniques to create that illusion. They use air-brush make-up for a flawless finish.

Airbrush make-up blends in perfectly with your skin so it looks like you haven't applied any make-up.

It conceals skin imperfections and hides blemishes, even major acne scars. It's fast and easy to apply - taking under a few seconds for the foundation to be applied all over your face and neck. It is long lasting as it can last up to 24 hours and is perspiration, water and transfer resistant. Air- brush make-up is very light and glides on to your skin as a natural make-up cover. Though it is an expensive alternative to your regular make-up but the result is far better than you can imagine. Sparmax and MAC Pro are few of the branded products for air-brush make-up available in India. So next time you see a celebrity don't feel threatened by their perfect make-up. It's quite possible that there is a layer of air-brush make-up; something that looks akin to their natural skin.

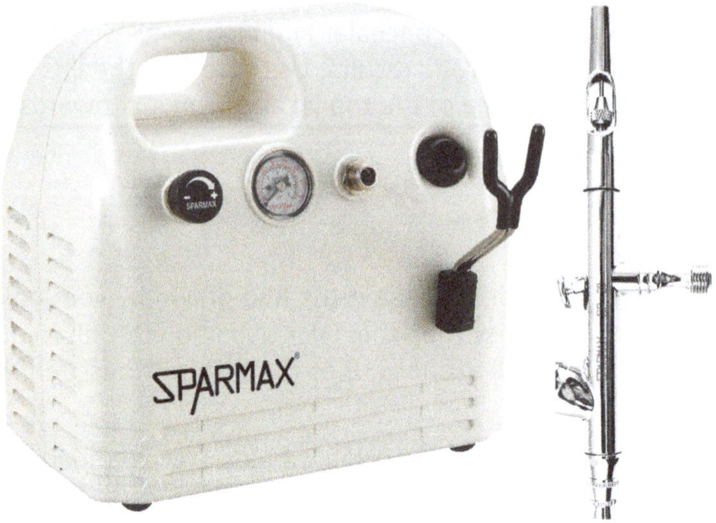

Air brush

Body make-up

Many are not blessed with a perfect skin. They have birth marks, burn scars, skin pigmentation, sun tan marks, and other skin discolouration on arms, legs, waist, back, neck, etc. Body make-up helps to make the skin tone even and create a flawless look. Body make-up is required to conceal scars, marks, and blemishes to achieve a perfect look.

There are many useful products available in the market to give your body ample glow and sheen. These products are well designed to cover most of the flaws with perfection. Tan sprays, bronzer, shimmer powders, body concealer, glosses, light reflective body oils, body glow, and air sprays are available to give you a super glam body.

If your veins show up at various places or you have a little scar on your knee from a childhood bruise or freckles on your arms; each one of these flaws can be camouflaged with the help of these products. At times body make-up is used to cover tattoos as well.

If you want to wear a two-piece swimsuit but are worried about the surgery mark on your waist, then you can apply water-resistant concealing spray or liquid make-up to cover up the mark. Even stretch marks can be taken care of with the help of body make-up.

You can create an even tone on all exposed parts of your skin with the help of loose mineral or light reflecting powder. Use the bronzer on your shoulders, back, or navel to achieve the glam goddess body look for a party.

Chapter Eleven

Make-up ideas for everyone

Make-up can make or break your look

Red carpet siren look

This look includes a flawless face with apt contouring and blush. Radiance and glow is the key. Use mineral powder instead of heavy foundation. For eyes, use earthy tones and nudes. Create a smudgy look around the eye-lines so that there are no defined lines. Apply one or two coats of mascara. Highlight the lips with bold and dark colours. All shades of red, plum, and wine can be used in lip lines and lipsticks.

Glamorous, red carpet look

Femme fatale look

It is timeless, beautiful and glamorous. It is an appropriate party or night time look. To achieve a Femme fatale-make-up look apply a liquid foundation and then correct all the flaws with a concealer or a corrector. Set the make-up with loose mineral powder. Add definition and subtle highlights to the cheekbones with sculpting powder or a blush in browns or darker shades. Create a vampy pout. Stick to the shades of reds, oranges and plums. Eyes should look dramatic and seductive. Use pastel shades to around the eye. Use dark eye liner to line near the lashes. Create voluminous eye lashes with two three coats of mascara. The brows should be well defined as well. Kohl or kajal can be applied to define the eyes well.

Femme fatale look

During daytime, create a milder version of this look with rose or salmon pink lips. Use subtle contouring and play down on eye make-up with lighter shades.

Rock chic look

Rock chic look

This look includes a heavy foundation to cover all flaws. Perfect contouring and dark blushers are used to create a chiselled look. Eyes are made dark and smokey. Shades of grey, black, purple, and dark browns are used to create, dark well-defined eyes with loads of mascara. The lips though, are kept nude with natural gloss. Depending on the time of the day, use the colour of the eye shadow. During daytime, use mild shades in browns, mauves, and greys. At night, use dark shades in black, deep grey, purple etc.

Natural/no make-up look

The no make-up is a quick, on-the-go look. It gives an effect of a luminescent complexion. To achieve a no-make-up look, apply a liquid foundation and then correct all the flaws with a concealer or a corrector. An under eye concealer is absolutely essential. Set it up with face powder or a loose mineral powder. Apply very little powder blush in plum or pink. Highlight the cheekbones for creating a chiselled look. Keep the lips luminous by applying gloss in shades of pink or plum. Highlight the softness and suppleness of your lips. The eyeliner should have a definite shape and try to use brown or dark brown eyeliner. Apply eye-shadow in shades of browns or chocolates. Apply little mascara to open up the eyes.

Natural look

Gothic look

Gothic look

This is a bold and heavy look. This look is tricky and you should be careful to match it up with your dress, accessories, and the occasion. This will include a heavy foundation and blush. Perfect contouring is done to create a chiselled look. Eyes are dark and well defined. Mascara, dark eye-shadows, and eyeliner are used generously. Lips are also dark and bold.

Gothic look is an evening look, perfect for parties and outings. Avoid it in daytime lest you would want to scare onlookers.

Good make-up can make a big difference in the way you look. It can also help to boost your self confidence. Glitches, on the other hand, can ruin all your efforts. A few make-up sins can make you look cakey and downright ugly. So be careful not to commit such make-up blunders; after all, well-applied make-up will boost your confidence to an astronomical level.

Chapter Twelve

Make-up sins

A good outside profile suggests that you are beautiful inside as well

Deadly make-up sins spell doom on your look, so avoid any mistakes while applying make-up. Ladies! I know a few of you would never want to apply any make-up on your face. You are just trying to project that you are not a high maintenance social butterfly, but looking neat with a bit of make-up does no harm. A little tinted moisturiser and a concealer goes a long way in creating a blemish-free skin tone. A bit of gloss and kajal will make you look bright and awake. And for parties, if you want, you may opt for professional help. Else, just be careful not to commit these mistakes.

Primer

A base or a canvas is required to put on make-up with finesse and beauty. Gel-based primers create a perfect base. Primer prepares your face to hold on to the make-up products for long and avoid frequent touch ups.

If you are not comfortable with primer, at least prepare your skin 5–10 minutes in advance with a light moisturiser. It will make your skin supple and you will feel that the make-up just glides on it.

Applying primer

Foundation

Choose the correct foundation. Don't go for oil-based foundation in summers. It will make your skin look very shiny. If you are not comfortable with applying daily foundation, use a tinted moisturiser.

Applying foundation

Choose the correct shade of foundation. Too dark and it will leave a tide mark around your face and neck, too light and it will make you look ghostly. Always pick a shade lighter than your skin tone or as specified to balance your face shape.

Mineral foundation is another alternative. A mineral powder foundation is easy to blend but make sure that the base is not too sticky. Use a light moisturiser to create a base.

Extend the application of foundation till your chest and neck. A uniform skin tone should be created in all these areas.

Avoid too much application of foundation to cover imperfections. It will make you look chalky. Instead, blend the foundation well and then hide the imperfections with a concealer.

Concealer

Choose the right shade of concealer. Usually concealers with yellow or salmon pink base are considered ideal. The skin under the eyes is thin. Heavy concealer on dark circle looks cakey. Keep it light and apply evenly with a brush. You can blend it with your fingertips as well. The best formula to apply concealer is to apply it over the foundation. First apply foundation, and later conceal uneven skin tone or blotches with the concealer.

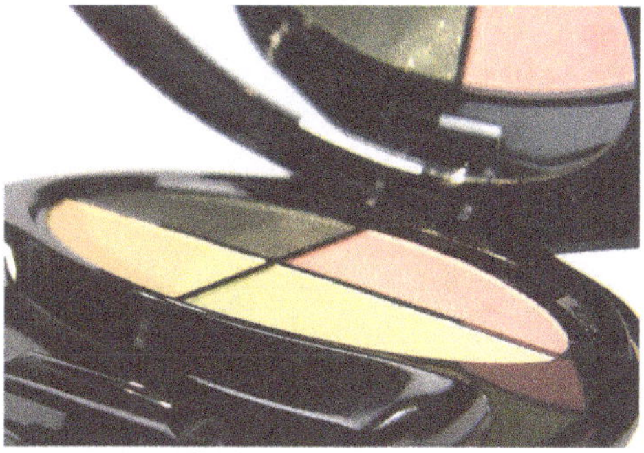

Applying concealer

Applying eyeliner

Eyeliner

Eyeliner should be applied close to the lash line. It should be smooth and even. But many who are not so experienced with eyeliners put it away from the lash line. They draw an uneven clumpy line. At times, the liner smudges on the skin near the brow. Make sure to apply the eyeliner properly.

If you are not very comfortable with a liquid liner, get pen liners which will be as easy as drawing a line with a sketch pen. If you are still not comfortable, get eye pencils. Eye pencils are a quick and easy way to draw a line near your lashes.

Kajal

Get a smudge- proof kajal. It is better to opt for a kajal which is smudge proof and water proof as with the very first touch or contact with water, the kajal starts bleeding, smudges out, and creates racoon eyes for you with resultant smudges all around your eyes and face. You don't want to look run down and Gothic.

Applying kajal

Eye-shadow

Applying eye-shadow

Use all colours provided in an eye-shadow palette. The lightest shade is to highlight near your brow line. The medium shade is to fill the entire body of your eye bulge, and the darkest should be applied around your lash line. Do not waste the colours. The palette has a purpose.

Don't opt for horizontal lines of eye-shadow. Always blend well. Make sure eye-shadow is not stuck between creases. Be careful while wearing a light shade near your lash line.

Mascara

A swipe of mascara on the lashes can open up any tired or droopy eye. It's the best beauty arsenal for women on the go who do not have time for an elaborate make-up ritual. But wrong application of the product can actually negate all the hard work.

The worst looking eyes are the ones that have sticky and clumpy mascara. Apply the mascara from the tip of the lash and work your way upwards. Drag the brush in a zigzag manner to avoid clumps. You can use an eyelash curler for a better effect.

Avoid mascara on the lower eyelashes. It highlights under eye dark circles and crow feet.

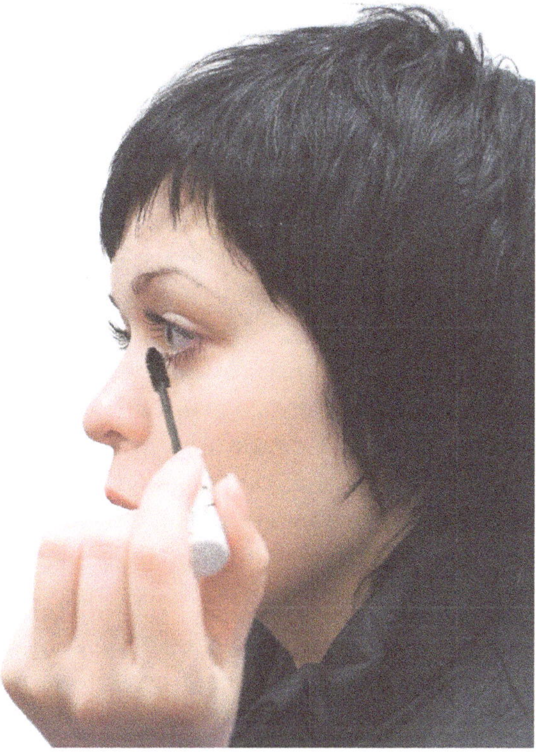

Applying mascara

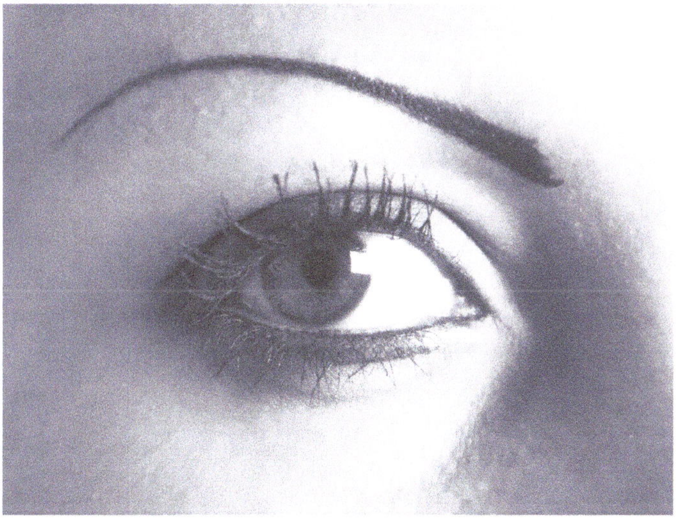

Over plucked eyebrow

Over plucked eyebrow

Over plucked eyebrow is a beauty disaster. Brows give definition to your face, but if your brows are plucked too thin, the natural beauty of the face is compromised.

Blush

Ancient Egyptians and Romans used various substances to give their cheeks a youthful and healthy pink glow. They used poppy and rose petals, red chalk, vermillion, red ochre, mulberry juice, wine dregs, cinnabar and red lead to get the pink hue. These days many convenient options are available in the market in powder, cream, and liquid forms. To get the best results, get a cream blush. It will give your cheeks a dewy effect. Powder blushes fade after a few hours but cream blushes stay on longer. Learn the exact skill of applying a blush. Do not just create rosy pink blotches on the apples of your cheek. Contour with angular strokes.

Never overdo blush. A peachy pink will give you a youthful glow and a brown would help you to contour. Avoid harsh pinks and browns.

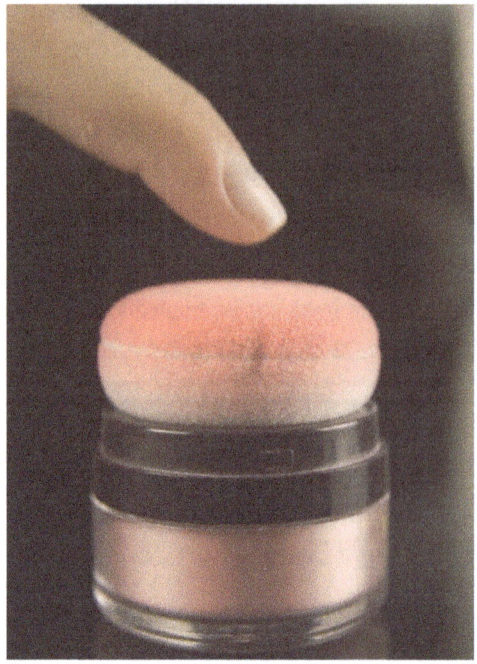

Blush

Lip liner

Lip liner

Too dark and harsh lip liners with light lipstick are an absolute no-no. They do not look good at all. Avoid it at all cost. In fact you just need a couple of lip liners for your entire make-up. A neutral or natural-coloured lip liner will take care of all your browns, peaches, and wine colour lipsticks. A red lip liner can take care of reds and corals. A natural pink will take care of your pink and mauve lipsticks.

Lipstick

Create a base for your lipstick or else it just gets wiped out in a couple of hours or bleeds down your lips, creating dirty blotches all over your face. Always use a primer or powder-based foundation to prepare your lips for lipstick.

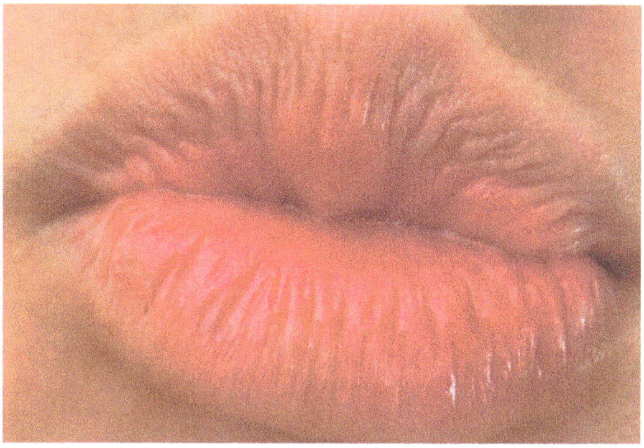

Don't apply lipstick on chapped lips

Never apply lipstick to chapped lips. Exfoliate the lips and then use a lip brush for perfect and smooth application.

Also, buy lipstick keeping in mind your skin tone. This way you will never look pale. Try to get non-transferable lipstick for longer staying power.

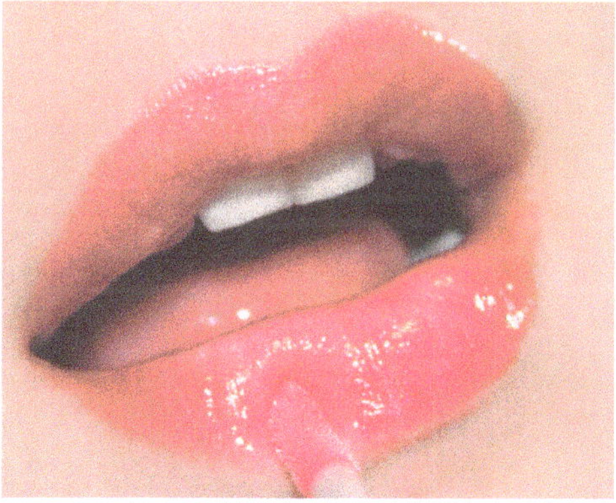

Lip-gloss

Lip-gloss

Avoid multiple coats of lip-gloss. Gooey lip-gloss looks very tacky and unappealing, especially in hot Indian weather.

Bronzer

Do not overdo bronzer lest you want to look like a brick. Bronzer helps to get you a sun-kissed glow. Apply it only to those areas where the sunlight would have touched you directly, like your forehead, your nose, and chin. Lightly dust it on these areas to get the perfect look.

Bronzer

Metallic and glitter make-up

Metallic and glitter make-up

Avoid it if you can. Keep it only for your costume parties. But if you are opting for metallic make-up, make sure to keep it subtle. A metallic white eye-shadow, with frost pink blush and a silver lipstick will make you look like an android. When using a golden eye-shadow, make sure it matches the occasion and your dress. Overdoing golden colour and glitter make-up will make you look like a walking Christmas present.

Pink and reds

Many women love pink and red as these are the colours for festivities. But overdoing any colour makes you look like a clown. Do not match your pink lipstick with a pink blush and a pink eye-shadow. It looks horrible.

Pinks and reds

Blues and greens

Navy blue, blue shadow, or dark green shadow

Use it with discretion as most of the times these highlight under eye dark circles.

Loose powder

When applying loose powder, don't be too generous with the application lest you want to look like Jerry mouse out of the flour bag. It will highlight the creases on the skin as well as make it look extremely dry. Be prudent and use it only where it is required.

Loose powder

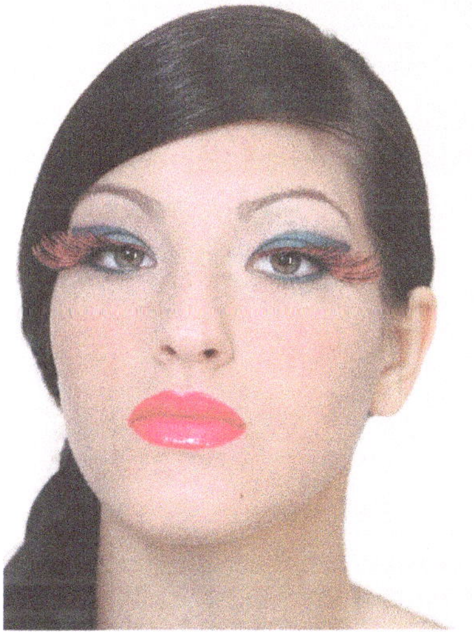

Overload of make-up

Overload of make-up

Never go overboard with make-up. You don't want to look made up with layers of foundation, eye-shadows, lipstick, and blush. Always highlight one feature at a time. If your lips are dark, keep the eyes subtle, if your eyes are dark, keep your lips subtle. Blusher is meant to contour and add a healthy flush to your cheeks. Do not overdo blush to create clown-like blotches.

Highlighter

Highlighter is an essential make-up product but its overuse can make your features look odd. It is usually applied under the brows to highlight the brow bones, or around the cheekbones. Too white and chalky or too light will do nothing to highlight your best feature. Make sure to use a good highlighter. Also, make sure you can see your skin through it.

Highlighter

Choose make-up as per time of the day

Daytime make-up is always light. Don't opt for smokey eyes during the day or even stark red lips during the day. Evening make-up is glamorous for you to use dark shades.

Daytime make-up

Bleaching of facial hair

Threading is better than bleaching hair as bleaching involves strong chemicals such as hydrogen peroxide that bleaches hair. Frequent use of such chemicals can make skin sensitive to sun and lead to concerns such as pigmentation. It can cause allergies, rashes, and aggravate other skin problems.

Also, bleaching does not benefit people with thick hair as the chemical in bleach makes hair brittle.

People with darker complexion do not benefit from bleaching as the golden look it gives to facial hair might contrast with the skin colour. Aesthetically too it looks tacky since hair is bleached, it does look lighter but when in light, the hair appears golden and it does not hide the hair on the face, making it obvious. Threading comparatively is safer, cleaner, and long lasting. Though, if you have very light facial hair, you can opt for natural or mild bleach.

Bleaching facial hair

Nail polish

Unshapely, dirty, and chapped nails look really messy. You might be decked up from top to bottom but if your nails are unclean and shabby, your true value goes drastically low. No woman can look her best with unflattering nails. You don't have to grow them enormously long. Just clean, neat and shapely nails will make you look your best. Varnish if you have to. Do not go by the trend and put on bright yellow or Sky blue nail polish. Choose subtle or clear varnish. Use emery boards to shape nails. Metal filers are not very beneficial as they damage the nail structure in the long run. You can use a buffer to give your nails a natural shine. Never apply a varnish coat on chapped nail polish. Always remove the old polish before applying a new coat of varnish. Go for manicures and pedicures regularly as it will help to keep a check on the overgrowth of cuticles. Or best, do it yourself at home. Get a manicure kit and follow the easy steps to give yourself a good home treatment. To make your hands look softer, use a sugar and lemon scrub for five minutes and then dip your hands in warm water for ten minutes.

Nail polish

If you avoid these small mistakes, you can be rest assured that your look will always warrant appreciative glances. A good outside profile suggests that you are beautiful inside as well. Most groomed and well-presented people have more popularity and friends. This is just a subjective observation, not necessarily completely true. But you can try to look your best and win hearts of the people around you.

Skin sins

We make so many skin sins on a daily basis. Going overboard with any skin care routine or ignoring any one is a major mistake. We help you stay aware and let you know the common goof ups.

Wax sin

Waxing is an effective method of removing unwanted hair from your body. Many opt for a regular arm and leg wax and at times face as well. But if the procedure is not done properly and hygienically, it may become the biggest skin sin.

Wax strips

The skin on the face is very sensitive and pulling and pushing during the waxing procedure may affect the elasticity of the facial skin.

Improper pulling or removal of hair may create painful zits on the skin. Dr. Preeti Savardekar, Consultant Dermatologist and Cosmetologist, Shri Krishna Polyclinic says, "Anyone suffering from diabetes and varicose veins or applying creams with Retin-A, Renova, Differin and Isotretinoin should be careful while using wax on their facial skin as their skin is too sensitive and prone to breakouts which will take a lot of time to heal. The precautions that they need to take while going for a wax is to stop applying Retinol based cream 2 days prior to waxing and also keep the skin well hydrated and moisturised. Start using Retinol based creams only after 2 days from the day you wax."

Too many facials, masks, and scrubs

Masks and scrubs

There are a variety of products available in the market to get you the best experience in facials, face masks and scrubs. In the hope of getting a flawless skin, a few over do the skin care routine which eventually backfires. Too many facials and massages affect the elasticity of your skin. Masks and scrubs help to remove dead cells from the skin.

Dr. Meha Mhatre, owner, Tressez Trichology & Advanced Skin Care Centre says, "Excessive exfoliation causes removal of living cells making the skin prone to easy damage and irritation." Exfoliate not more than twice a week for a healthy skin. Facial and masks are good not more than twice a month.

Using masks too often will make your skin very dry as it rips off natural oils and moisture from the skin. Scrubs are abrasive and using them too often will damage the skin as facial tissues are quite delicate.

Make-up brushes and sponge

Using dirty make-up, brushes and sponge

Unclean make-up, brushes and applicators are home to many bacteria and viruses. How often do we clean them? May be once in a while! And when we apply make-up with these on our skin, both skin and the make-up products become a breeding ground for the germs. Try to clean your make-up brushes and sponges at regular intervals with mild soap and hot water to keep them germ free. Make sure they are absolutely dry before reusing them.

Forgetting to tone

Cleansing and moisturising our skin is a regular habit for many. But toning takes a back seat or rather ignored completely. For a youthful and happy skin, all three are equally important. Toning compliments cleansing as it removes dirt, excess oil and dead cells from the skin which help to avoid blemishes and break outs. A toner refines and tightens pores giving the skin a radiant and fresh complexion. Cleansing, toning and moisturising are a must in your daily skin care routine.

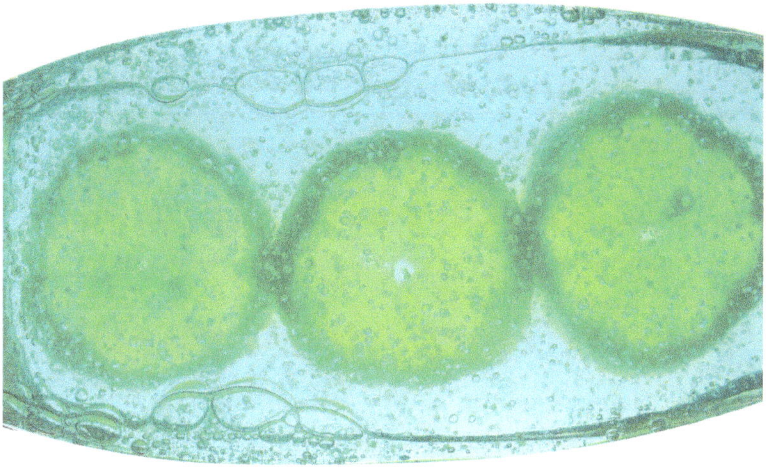

Forgetting to tone

Face lifting and Botox sin

Non-invasive face lifts like 'Thermage' and Botox are getting popular day by day as these procedures are painless and result oriented. Botox is a prescription medicine that is injected into muscles to get rid of wrinkles and frown-lines. 'Thermage' uses radio waves to help build collagen in our skin and make it tight. But too much of anything is bad for your skin. People as young as in late 20's are getting such procedures done and that too at frequent intervals. This may disrupt the growth of normal healthy cells and your facial skin may become completely dependent on the external help to look taut and young. Be prudent while opting for such procedures and limit the usage.

Let yourself avoid such drastic sins, to have a glowing and beautiful skin. With proper care, you can enjoy a flawless skin forever.

Chapter Thirteen

Beauty care and non-invasive face lifts

Glowing and clear skin is coveted by all as it is a sign of health and beauty

Enhance skin texture

Many of you have always coveted a flawless complexion and a youthful glow. You can get that by paying attention to your health and following a strict beauty regime. You can begin safeguarding your skin against the increased pollution and the stress your skin bears due to exposure to sunlight by regularly applying a good moisturizer and sunscreen. This helps fight dryness in the air, pollution, and UV rays. You should use a sunscreen lotion which has SPF (Sun Protection Factors) level 30 at least. Your sunscreen lotion bottle should read protects from UVA + UVB rays 'Ultra Violet Ageing and Ultra Violet Burning'.

Go for facials, peels, and gentle exfoliation as it helps to get luminous complexion and keeps your pores free from pollutants, dirt, and grime in the air.

Cleanse and tone your skin regularly to keep it healthy and supple. Have plenty of water for a healthy skin as it flushes out toxins and keeps the fluids of the body running efficiently.

Avoid sugary and fried foods which are in abundance, as digesting sugar leads to a process known as glycation that damages collagen and elastin, adding years to your looks and also gives rise to boils, pimples, and rashes.

Smoking and alcohol intake also make your skin dry and aged.

Munching on colourful, nutrient-rich fruits and vegetables improves skin's radiance. So include maximum portions of fresh fruits and vegetables in your diet.

Exercise and a good sleep are the easiest ways to achieve a radiant skin. Indulge in cardio exercises to get the oxygen in your blood moving. Skin keeps on regenerating itself throughout the day, but it is slightly faster at night. So get uninterrupted 7-8 hours of sleep every night for a luminous skin.

Let yourself shine and glow and get better with each passing day by following these simple rules.

Know your creams

Time and again you are reminded to use good creams and sunscreens. In fact experts recommend using good products all the time. What are the various ingredients in these creams? Know them now before you purchase a cream off the shelf:

Today the market is flooded with various skin products. We all hear about certain ingredients used in these such as vitamin E, AHA (Alpha Hydroxic Acid), Niacin amide B3 complex, retinol, SPF, etc. But what are their benefits?

Skin experts confirm that skin products do work. Customers who use anti-ageing creams after they see skin damage like fine lines, wrinkles, blemishes, etc. feel disheartened as no substantial results show. Anti-ageing creams and most of the skincare products are for prevention.

Start using anti-ageing creams by the age of 25, to prolong the onset of aging of your skin.

Let us understand anti-ageing ingredients. Dr Preeti Savardekar shares her expertise:

Anti-ageing products helps in skin cell rejuvenation and to build collagen and elastin. Collagen and elastin gives our skin the elasticity and plumpness for youthful appearance. The ingredients helpful in building collagen are AHA(Alpha Hydroxy Acid), Retinol, Coenzyme Q10 and to a certain extent Allantoin.

Retinol is the best ingredient to effectively fight the signs of ageing. Retinol is a form of vitamin A that is also found naturally in our skin. Retinol stimulates the renewal and repair processes in skin including the production of elastin and collagen, helping the skin to repair itself and be bouncy and firm.

Conjugated Linoleic Acid helps to stimulate natural cell turnover. It has lipid factors useful especially for older skin as it helps to hydrate and nourish the skin.

AHA (Alpha Hydroxy Acid) is a salt to weaken bonds of old and dead skin cells from the outer layer of the skin and help in skin renewal.

Allantoin also has the anti-ageing properties but not many creams use this ingredient as it needs a very fine balance with others to give effective results.

Now let us also know about the rejuvenating, skin lightening, or healing ingredients used in skin products.

Rejuvenating products are those which have hydrating, soothing, and healing properties. Pro-Vitamin B3, Niacin amide B3 complex, Vitamins A, C, and E, and SPF help in skin nourishment, softening, and protection.

Vitamins A, C and E help in nourishing and moisturising the skin. They help in the healing process after chemical peels or other damage to the skin.

Pro-Vitamin B3 helps in the deep moisturizing of the skin. It helps to soften the skin and gives boost to plumpness and suppleness of the skin.

Niacin amide B3 complex helps in reducing pigmentation, helps in skin lightening, soothing, and healing of the skin.

SPF (Sun Protection Factor) helps the skin against sun damage due to UVA and UVB rays. SPF 30 or more is recommended to protect your skin against harsh sun ray damage.

Next time you invest in a skincare product, make sure you know the ingredients involved and the benefits you will get when you use them.

Skin around the eyes

Fresh and beautiful eyes always command attention. With your busy routine and unhealthy lifestyle (read eyes glued to TV screens or laptop/ computer monitors for long hours), it is not surprising that eyes look dull and tired. And eventually signs of ageing are visible on your precious set, quicker than ever. Under eye dark circles, bags under your eyes, redness in eyes, and crow feet are common signs and are a big cause of concern for many. Invest in good rejuvenating creams which will help you counter the ageing and dullness.

The skin around the eyes is the most delicate as the fat tissues start losing their vitality faster than any other area on the face, leaving signs of ageing and exhaustion. Moreover, the effects of dry weather, cold, heat, and sun damage make your precious set look beaten outright. Invest in eye creams or smoothing serums which can give your eyes maximum hydration and a supple look. Mac's Moisture Lush Eye Cream is the perfect buy for this purpose. As well as Olay Regenerist Eye Lifting Serum which has concentrated amino-peptide + B3 complex to help firm and lift skin around the eye. Always look for non-greasy and fragrance-free products to avoid irritation around the eyes.

Vitamin C, E, and hydrolysed proteins are the potent contributors to healthy and fresh-looking eyes as they are effective anti-aging ingredients. They help in skin elasticity and collagen production. Hydrolysed proteins help in correcting and rejuvenating the skin. Lotus Herbals Nutraeye gel is enriched with these qualities.

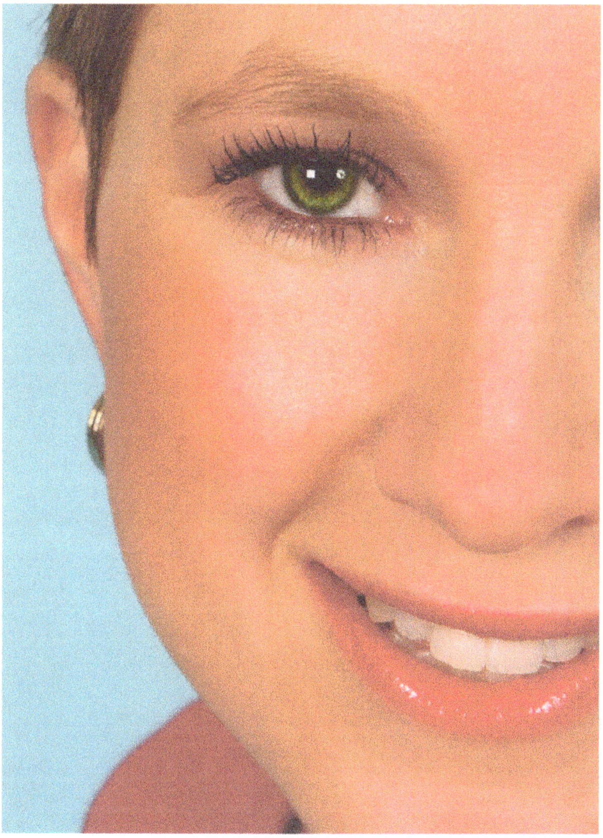

Delicate skin around the eyes

Don't forget to remove your eye make-up with a gentle oil-based make-up remover before going to bed. It's also important to look after the health and cleanliness of your peepers to keep them beautiful forever.

Chemical peels

Chemical peels are used to treat skin problems on the face. Uneven skin tone, wrinkles, blemishes, skin pigmentation and acne are treated with chemical peels. Chemical peel uses a chemical solution to improve the texture of the facial skin. It removes the damaged outer layers or the top layer of the skin so that a new skin layer can regenerate. The new skin is smoother than the older one. It helps to get an even skin tone by removing scars, pigments, and other skin discolourations. A chemical peels are used to achieve radiant glow and a youthful skin.

Dr. Rohini Wadhwani, Cosmetologist and Medical Director, Skin Essentials, says, 'Peels can be very beneficial to the skin if used correctly. We see excellent results in those suffering from acne and pigmentation and results can be seen from the very first treatment.'

Some of the other benefits seen with peels include:

- Softens and smoothens the skin.
- Reduces fine lines and wrinkles as it rejuvenates the skin's collagen.
- Re-hydrates dry/dull complexions, making skin more youthful.
- Helps with acne and pigmentation because of its exfoliating properties.

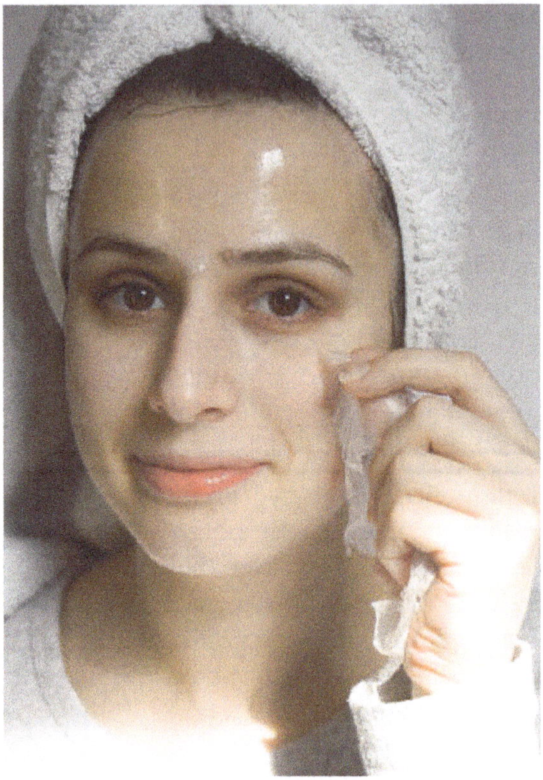

Skin peels

A thorough consultation should be carried out with the doctor to determine the type of peel, strength, suitability, and rule out any contraindications to the treatment. Hence, it is very important to see a doctor and not an aesthetician for this procedure. Peels vary in their strength and may be superficial, medium, or deep.

Dr. Neha Mhatre, Tressez Trichology & Advanced Skincare Centre says,

'Peels are usually beneficial but if the process is not followed properly, it can backfire.'

Some of the drawbacks

- Persistent redness may occur and can last for months. It makes the skin very sensitive and any long duration of sun exposure may result in rashes or redness.
- If proper post care is not taken, it might result in skin infection, irritation and burning. After peel, do not use excessive hot water, soap on skin for at least 48 to 72 hours. Do not exercise as salt in the sweat might irritate the skin.

- ☞ Peeling and burning of the skin after the chemical peel may cause inconvenience if not done with proper care and understanding.
- ☞ Sunscreen needs to be applied religiously after the chemical peel as the problem may return with higher intensity. Apply a sunscreen with a minimum of SPF 30, fifteen minutes prior to stepping out and re-applied every 3 to 4 hrs.
- ☞ Anyone using a Vitamin A derivative cream or medication should give a 6-month gap for chemical peel after stopping the medication as peels make the skin dry and so does the medication. This might lead the skin to dry excessively.
- ☞ Open wounds have to be treated before going for a peel or it might lead to infection.
- ☞ People with Keloidal tendencies must take appropriate care.
- ☞ The results of chemical peels are temporary and do not substitute surgery. Treatments might have to be repeated.

Any procedure, if not followed properly, will not yield the desired results. Do your homework well and assess the pros and cons before resorting to the chemical peels.

Botox and Galvanic treatment

A picture perfect look with a flawless skin is dreamt by every woman. Everybody wants a magic potion that can undo the fine wrinkles, lines and pores on the skin. Galvanic treatment and Botox are the two remedies to answer this plight.Botox or Botulinum toxin 'A' injections are used to treat laugh lines, crow's feet, frown lines, etc., to get a more youthful look. This is a form of serum which is injected in the lower layers of the skin, which make skin cells plump and in the process reduce wrinkles.

Galvanic treatment is a procedure where a massager is used, which uses galvanic ions or ultrasound waves or a combination of both to treat the skin. An essential nourishing cream is massaged deep into the skin using this massager. Ultrasonic waves promote the growth of healthy skin and boost elasticity. It is safe to be used on problem skin with acne, pimples, and blackheads.

Dr. MehaMhatre, Trichologist, Skin Specialist and Owner, Tressez Trichology & Advanced Skincare Centre, says:

Botox and Galvanic treatment

'Galvanic treatment helps in removing skin wastes and aids cosmetic nutrients to penetrate deep into the skin by applying galvanic ions and ultrasound waves. It helps activate skin cells and tissues through a million micro vibrations per second. It also helps in reducing wrinkles, sagging skin, and is recommended for firming and lifting the skin by using the anode (+) and the cathode (-) of electric currents. Here are some of the additional benefits:

- It helps the growth of healthy skin with more elasticity all over the face.
- It improves blood circulation in the facial skin.
- The possible side effects of this treatment are increase in skin sensitivity for a while after the procedure is completed.

Dr. Preeti Savardekar, Consultant Dermatologist & Cosmetologist of Shri Krishna Polyclinic, says:

- Botox is used to treat lines and wrinkles at a target area on the face like frown-lines, crow feet and laugh lines. It doesn't treat the overall look of the skin on the face.
- Botox, if not administered properly may result in disorders with muscle weakness like multiple sclerosis, amyotrophic lateral sclerosis.

- Botox may cause allergies, swelling, bruising, infections and headaches which may not be a good experience.
- Botox treatments are temporary. The effect starts wearing off within three to four months. Somebody who wants to sustain the effect all year long may have to visit the clinic regularly.

Galvanic treatment is better than Botox therapy as galvanic treatment is a safer and more effective way of reducing fine lines and wrinkles. Though it doesn't target a particular area; galvanic treatment helps in promoting a healthier skin with improved elasticity all over the face. As a result it makes the skin look younger and taut. Botox should be used for removing deep wrinkles in a target area like frown lines, crow's feet, laugh lines etc.

Thermage skin firming treatment

There are times when you wish that you could turn back the time and make your wrinkles disappear. This might be possible in fiction but in real life beauty treatments like 'Thermage skin firming' come to your aid in acquiring youthful skin. A non-invasive procedure for skin tightening and contouring, it also diminishes fine lines and wrinkles in the process.

Thermage skin firming treatment

The 'Thermage skin firming' is a safe, non-surgical procedure used for face lifting and tightening skin in other areas of the body as well. Dr. Rohini Wadhwani, Director, Skin Essentials says, "A protein called collagen makes up the majority of the dermis (the deeper layer of the skin), providing the skin with its strength. As we become older, the body produces less collagen and the skin becomes less elastic, resulting in wrinkles. 'Thermage skin firming' procedure tightens the collagen in the dermal layers of the skin and its underlying tissue, thus reducing loose skin and wrinkles and rejuvenating facial contours."

Before starting the procedure, a cooling spray is used on the skin in order to protect its top layers from damage. A 'Thermacool wand' apparatus is used to emit radio frequency waves for stimulating the collagen layer under the skin. Patients can see a visible difference in the very first treatment, witnessing a more youthful glow and firmness. The effect of the treatment stays on for several months. The cost though varies per treatment. A quotation is given only after a skin analysis is undertaken by the specialist. (This could be anywhere between Rs 2500 – Rs 5000 or above.)

It usually takes an hour or even lesser to complete the process depending on the condition of the skin that needs to be treated. One of the major benefits of this treatment is that there are no real discernible signs or scars and the downtime and recovery is minimal. With better services and equipments, this procedure rarely has any side effects. Though, a few reported side effects are redness, swelling, numbness and blisters. Slight warming tinges and sensations may be felt during the treatment.

Make sure that the treatment is undertaken by expert hands. Do not consume alcohol before or after the treatment. Alcohol disturbs blood circulation which can make the treatment less effective. Intake of aspirin or any other drug with vitamin E is also not recommended before the treatment, as it might lead to bruises in the treatment area. If you are pregnant or suffer from any other illness, discuss the condition in advance with the specialist before going for the treatment. Do not undergo any other facial treatment after Thermage skin firming, till authorized by your specialist. Use good skin creams and sunscreens after the treatment to maintain the improved skin structure for long.

Beauty and science can certainly deliver wonders and 'Thermage skin firming' proves it right. There are many other ways to improve the look of your skin. You need to be conscious while dealing with your skin to make it appear young and beautiful for long.

Laser photo rejuvenation treatment

Laser makes the skin firmer and smoother. De-pigmenting creams are massaged in the skin with specially designed machines. Post that Vitamin enriched creams are used along with hydration and skin brightening packs to treat the facial skin. Its effect lasts for a few years and within a few sittings you see a big difference in your skin's appearance. It reduces wrinkles, treats sun spots and visible veins, tightens loose skin, improves skin tone and complexion. There is no recovery time involved, it induces reduced pore size, redness and even skin texture. Skin experts say that it is really effective on mature skin.

There are many such non-surgical procedures which can help you turn back time; but of course, only for a few years. We cannot escape from the age that soon catches up from time to time. You can only perhaps choose to delay the onset of aging process by following any of these treatments.

Exotic facials

We all know about the regular facials available in the parlours. A few exotic ones can be a good change from your routine.

To keep your face youthful and fresh, pamper it with a wide range of exotic facials offered by well known Spas and beauty clinics.

Here are a few Exotic facials listed for you:

Dark chocolate facials

Chocolate lovers have a new reason to rejoice! If the whiff of raw cocoa tempts you to eat the product than apply, please curb your appetite. Cocoa powder is the highest known natural source of magnesium and antioxidants. It also contains vitamins A, B1, C, D, and E which are good for skin. Antioxidants absorb free radicals, that cause cell and tissue damage; the rogues that are responsible for premature aging. Such a facial improves the appearance of sun damage, fine lines and signs of aging. It also has de-tanning properties.

Side effect: Dr Preeti Savardekar of Shri Krishna Polyclinic cautions that chocolate facial may cause breakouts, if you are allergic to chocolate and milk products. Cost – Rs 800/ and above. (Price subject to change in future)

Dark chocolate facial

Pearl, silver, gold, gems and diamond facials

Since ancient times, natural gems and minerals have been a source of beauty. Kings and queens knew that items in their treasure were not only good as ornaments but to beautify as well. In various parts around the globe like Japan, Egypt, Rome, Greece etc. minerals have been used to gain beauty since a very long time. Pearls, gold and silver facials are still popular in many parts of the world. What are the qualities which make these minerals so popular? Let's find out.

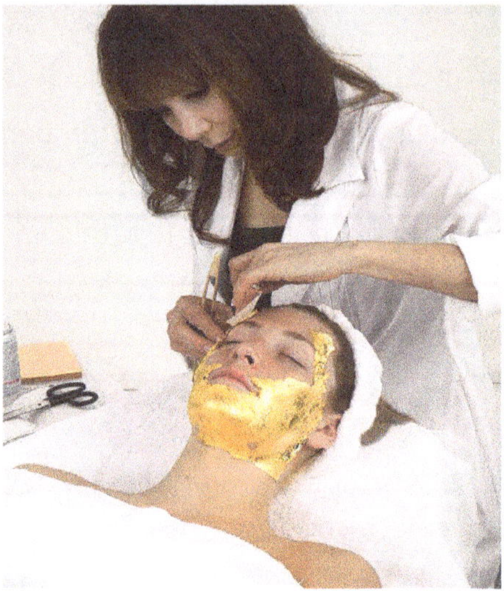

Gold facial

Silver detoxifies and purifies the skin. Pearls are naturally rich in amino acids, minerals, and proteins that have powerful age control properties. This also helps in skin brightening and reduces blemishes and dark spots.

Gold slows down collagen depletion and the breakdown of elastin to prevent sagging skin. A gold facial stimulates cellular growth and helps to regenerate healthy, firm skin cells. It also reduces the appearance of fine lines and wrinkles. Ash of gems like ruby is used to give a cooling and soothing effect to the skin.

Diamond facials are more of micro-dermabrasion and skin polishing. A diamond wand which has an array of "diamond" crystals is used to polish the skin and leave it luminous and radiant. The procedure is used to diminish blackheads and white heads, fine lines, acne scarring, enlarged pores, lip and character lines and stretch marks.

Side effect: Diamond facials can be done only by an expert and are very costly. Pearl, Silver, Gem and Gold facials are not advised for acne prone and sensitive skin as this may worsen the skin condition. Cost – varies.

Caviar and wine facial

Dr. Rohini Wadhwani of Skin essential says that, "The wine based products are filled with anti-oxidants and the red grape skin and seeds are full of polyphenols and resveratrols for cell renewal to help your skin stay fresh and young." It is best for dry and sensitive skin. It helps to extract toxins and impurities from the skin. It promotes cell regeneration hence slowing normal aging process. It deeply moisturizes and smoothes skin. It also uses honey which is a natural skin firming agent and increases elasticity.

Wine facial

Caviar

Side effect: There are no side effects as natural and gentle ingredients are used. Though, it is an expensive treatment as heritage wines are costly. Cost - Rs 2400/ - (price subject to change in future.)

Collagen and sea algae facial

Dr Meha Mhatre of Tressez Trichology and Advanced skin care suggests ingredients like Collagen, Sea Algae, Milk Extracts, etc., for this facial. It works best for mature skin, dark circles, fine lines & wrinkles and helps to cleanse, nourish, hydrate and contour facial skin. It is rich in minerals such as zinc, copper, iron, silicone and magnesium etc., those minerals that play an important role in the health of skin.

Collagen and sea algae facial

Side effect: A test should be performed prior to the facial to ascertain that there is no allergy from collagen otherwise it may result in skin reddening, bruising, peeling and itching. Cost – Rs 1850 (price subject to change in future.)

Chapter Fourteen

Accessories

Right accessories can make a lot of difference to enhancing your overall look

Accessorize and you can create different looks with a single dress. Bags, scarves, belts, shades, hats and jewellery are the popular ways to accessorize. Accessorizing helps us hide our flaws and highlight the best. While we think a lot while choosing a dress or shoes, little attention is given to our bag, belt, shades, jewellery, etc.

Not much effort is put into scrutinising the length of the necklace, the size of the bag, the colour of the hat or scarf.

The right accessories can make a lot of difference to enhancing your overall look.

Handbags

Let us focus on the most important accessory. You have guessed it right! The handbag. An extension to your personality, your handbag reflects a lot about your lifestyle and taste. Handbags are available in leather, patent leather, fabric, good quality plastic and other products. The question here is what could possibly go wrong with a handbag? As long as it looks good and is able to carry everything that is needed by a woman, it should be just fine. Well 'just fine' is not what you are aiming at; you are darting for that perfect look. So here are a few pointers in choosing a good hand bag:

☞ A good handbag can help to knock off pounds visually. You heard it right! If you are voluptuous and short choose a handbag which looks tall, slender and angular. A clutch is the best option. But if you want to choose a bag, go for mid size rectangular bags.

Handbags

- If you are tall and slim look for a rounded, slouchy hobo bag. A rounded and unshapely bag will add volume to your structure.
- A bag should be in proportion to your body. If you are tall as well as voluptuous, a tiny bag will look lost in the giant frame. If a very slim and short woman is carrying a very large slouchy bag, it will look overbearing on her petite frame.
- Use bag to highlight your best feature. If you want to focus on your hip, the length of your bag should be long enough to touch your hips. If you want to focus on your waist, the length of your bag should be around your waist. Most women look great with a bag that is mid length or is around mid torso because it flatters the waist.
- Carry bags according to your outfit. A summer floral dress will not look good with a black work bag.

- ☞ Choose an essential day bag in brown as goes with almost all the colours of your dresses and accessories.
- ☞ Choose an essential day bag in black as it goes with (the colours) Black, White, Gray and Taupe. Do not carry a black bag with all your dresses.
- ☞ Choose an essential fabric bag with beads and sequins for a dinner or an outing in the evening.
- ☞ Choose an essential party bag in Silver, Gold or Diamante. Match it with your jewellery.
- ☞ Choose an essential travel bag which can also serve as your weekend bag. This is one bag you can carry on board a flight.
- ☞ Choose an essential wallet or a purse bag for the days when you need to carry bare essentials like keys, cards, phone, etc.
- ☞ Never over stuff your bag with a lot of things. It should not seem that you are carrying the whole world in your handbag. Buy small size make-up and beauty products, foldable hair brush and other compact items.

Some popular shapes

1. Tote – An open-top bag with straps or handles
2. Hobo bag – A crescent-shaped shoulder bag
3. Duffle – Tall shoulder bag, often with a wider opening on top
4. Field bag – A flap-top shoulder bag with utility-type closure (buckles, snaps, etc)
5. Clutch – A small, handheld bag or a larger, geometric shape that is tucked under the arm
6. Satchel – A large, handheld bag
7. Baguette – Long and rounded shoulder bag resembling the Baguette bread.
8. Messenger – A large, soft shoulder bag with long straps (often worn across the body)
9. Pouch – A soft, small bag
10. Hermes style bag – A classic large, structured handbag with distinctive hardware closures
11. Cross body bag: It is worn across body like a Messenger bag but is more lady-like and elegant. It might resemble a clutch or it may be bigger than a clutch

Fashion scarves

Fashion scarves are another great way to accessorize. You can cover your head, use it as a head band, tie it around your neck or simply let it hang with your handbag. It just peps up the ensemble all together.

Fashion scarves are commonly made from silk, rayon or acetate, offering light weight, fluid movement, strength, and a shimmering finish. Other common fabrics for scarves are cotton and wool, which make for a slightly heavier scarf, with structure and often textured finishes. Scarves come in various shapes and sizes; many designed for specific uses. There are bandanas and kerchiefs that range from a smaller size to large shawl-like scarves. There are square scarves, rectangular (or oblong) scarves, and triangular scarves. Some scarves have hemmed edges, fringed edges, and fused edges. They are available in various prints and woven patterns, both in neutral and solid colours. In short, the possibilities are endless with fashion scarves. So why not choose the right scarf to enhance your looks.

Scarf

Here are a few pointers

- If you are short and little over weight and want to wear a long scarf, wear one in a light knit like woven silk.
- You can use your scarf to hide your untidy hair by wearing it as a head band.
- If you have short and fat neck, wear the scarf wrapped around the neck to create an elongating effect.
- If you have long neck, wear your scarf in loop or tied around your neck.
- If you have wrinkled or discoloured neck, wear scarf as a choker to hide the flaws.
- Wear your scarf as a belt. Wear it with a plain dress or shirt and simply wrap it with a twist around your waist. Using a contrasting colour or pattern will make you look sensational.

Belts

Belt

Belts are not just the objects which hold your trouser in place; they have the capacity to add an element of fun if you choose the right piece. Belts are worn not only on trousers but jeans, dresses and even coats. Belts can create a waist if you don't have one or make your derriere look smaller if you select the right piece. Belts are available in various styles and designs. Leather, patent leather, plastic and fabric belts are the ones that are most popular. A stretchable fabric gives you the flexibility to use a single belt in different places with different dresses. You can be really creative with this piece of accessory.

The two things that you should keep in mind while choosing a good belt is the width of the belt and the buckle size.

These two factors make a lot of difference in the way you look. Focus on your bone structure, instead of your weight while choosing a belt.

- ☞ If you have thin bone structure, then keep the buckle small and delicate. If you have medium bone structure then medium sized buckle should be fine. If you have large bone structure then large buckle would be perfect.
- ☞ Similarly, heavy boned women should avoid wearing skinny belts. It will be lost on their body frame.
- ☞ Big breasted women should not wear big buckles as this will look over crowded at the front.
- ☞ Big derriere would need broad hipster belts to make them look smaller. Wear it low on your waist.
- ☞ When you are wearing one coloured dress from head to toe, don't break the monochrome effect with a different coloured belt.

Fashion jewellery

Fashion jewellery is another big element in adding a bit of zing to your look. We pick up pieces which we find attractive without thinking that how will it look once we wear it. Here are a few pointers that will help you choose the right jewellery.

Fashion jewellery

- ☞ If you have short neck, broad face and big breasts, then wear delicate pieces. Statement necklaces will look unflattering on you. Big breasted women can wear tear shaped delicate pendants to look elegant.
- ☞ If you are heavy around your jaw line or have a double chin, avoid statement neckpieces.
- ☞ Long necks can wear choker like necklaces as well as statement neckpieces. But avoid very thin choker as it will elongate your neck further.
- ☞ Never wear lots of gold chains or bling unless you want to ape a rap star.
- ☞ Do not wear a statement neck piece and heavy earrings or dangling earrings together, until they are part of a set.
- ☞ Chains and pendants over polo neck look unpleasant.
- ☞ Slash neck lines should not be accompanied with necklaces. Wear statement earrings instead.
- ☞ Oval or oblong faces look good in chandelier shaped earrings. They can easily carry off studs too.
- ☞ Pear studs look fab with a lady like dress, but look dull as daily wear.
- ☞ Long diamante danglers are only good for a party. Do not use them in daily wear jewellery.
- ☞ Round and dangling earrings makes a round face and chin look slimmer. Round faces should avoid studs or round clip-on earrings.

- ☞ Short necks look shorter with long dangling earrings. Wear medium size earrings or studs.
- ☞ For office or for a professional look, wear studs. And if they don't suit you, then go for a bracelet or a delicate neckpiece instead of earrings.
- ☞ Slender and shapely fingers should opt for delicate and small designs in rings.
- ☞ Do not wear too many rings at one go. One piece other than your engagement band is more than enough.
- ☞ Thick and short fingers can opt for longer designs. This helps to elongate your fingers.
- ☞ Cocktail rings should be worn only in cocktail parties or dinner. Don't wear them during the day.
- ☞ Thin bones should opt for delicate bracelets and large bones can easily carry chunky bracelets.

Watches

Watches not only state time but also help you to make a style statement. Watches are an important fashion accessory and have a great influence on the overall look that you want to project. Many people dismiss the use of watches. They are of the opinion that if you possess a cell phone, you don't really need a watch. The purpose of keeping track of time is already being addressed by cell phones. But watches are more like those elegant and exquisite bracelets that lift up your mood and rev up your look in a fraction of a second. There are various designs to choose from in both link chain and leather band. Big dials, small dials, chronograph dials, fabric wrist bands, bracelet bands and a lot more choices are available with various brands. The two essential pieces that you should have is a watch in leather wrist band and the other in link chain band.

Watch

Whenever you choose a dial, always consider your bone structure. Choosing a watch is to choosing a bracelet.

Here are a few pointers to help you choose the right watches:

- Thin bones should opt for delicate watches and large bones can easily carry chunky watches with big dials. Large dials are very fashionable these days unless they look bulbous and too large on your wrist. Wear watches according to your bone structure.
- Leather watches should fit well on your wrist. Do not tie it lose that it keeps on slipping on your wrist. It looks very unkempt and tacky. Link chain bands can be a bit loose.
- Frayed, discoloured and torn leather bands should be replaced. Discoloured or rusted link bands should be replaced as well. Keep your watch clean.
- Fashion watches should be worn only at casual occasions. Don't wear a diamante studded watch to your office.
- Wear your watch in contrast to your dress. Don't wear a black leather band with a black dress or a pink fabric band with your pink T-shirt. Instead wear a white leather band with black dress or blue fabric band with your pink T-shirt.
- Match the colour of your watch with your shoes and bag.
- Wear unisex design watches with casual wear like T-shirt and jeans. Do not team it up with your business suit or traditional attire like saree.
- Be very careful when you are wearing a golden link watch with a black dial. This combination doesn't go too well with many colours.

Sunglasses

Sunglasses

Good quality sunglasses are your eye's best friend and a stylish pair of sunglasses will make you look like a star. People have become conscious about the damage done by UVA & UVB rays to our skin and eyes. To protect the eyes from any further sun damage, these days many invest in good quality sunglasses.

Sunglasses not only protect your eyes but also make you look stylish. Simply consider the shape of your face while choosing the right sunglasses. Here are a few pointers to choose the right frame for your peepers:

Oval face: As you have mostly balanced proportions, chin is narrower than forehead most frame shapes will look good on you. You can choose square, rectangular, geometrical shapes that add angles to your facial curves.

Avoid: Frames that are too large for your features should be avoided at all cost.

Heart face: As you have a broad forehead and wide cheekbones with a narrow chin, bottom heavy frames are best suited for you as they will add width to your lower face. Wear styles with low set temples to draw attention downwards. Use narrow and round frames that soften the forehead.

Avoid: Top-heavy styles that draw attention upwards and decorative temples that accentuate the broad forehead should be avoided.

Triangle face: As you have narrow forehead and wider cheeks and chin semi-rimless frames will help accentuate the upper face. These are best suited for you. Top-heavy styles that balance the width of the jaw will also look great on you.

Avoid: Low set temples that widen the jaw or narrow frames that are out proportion should be avoided.

Square face: As you have an angular face with a strong jaw line, broad forehead and square chin, Oval and round frames will balance your face shape. Glasses with temples that are centre set or that connect at the top of the frame are best suited for your face shape.

Avoid: Geometric Square shaped frames that highlight your angular face structure. Low set temples or colour accents on the bottom of the frames that draw emphasis to the chin.

Round face: As you have full cheeks, rounded chin and have a face whose width and length are almost same, angular and geometric shapes are best for you as they will help to sharpen the facial structure. Rectangular and horizontal frames will make your face appear longer and slim. Frames with temples that connect at the top of the frame will add length to your face.

Avoid: Round frames and large frames should be avoided as they will make your face appear shorter and rounder.

Rectangular or oblong face: As you have a proportionally longer face from forehead to chin and the width of your cheekbones is less, tall frames that help create a shorter face are ideal for you. Choose frames with an accented top rim or decorative temple that adds width to your face.

Avoid: Avoid small frames that are not proportionate or short frames that accentuate the length of your face.

There are many other accessories like gloves, pins, brooches,hair-bands, hair-pieces, leg warmers, leggings, stockings and tights which are used to supplement your apparel. Smart application of these accessories enhances your appeal and makes you look gorgeous. So pay attention to your accessories next time you go shopping. The next important factor is the pair of shoes you wear. Let us find out more about the essential pairs and how to choose the right pair for your feet.

Chapter Fifteen

Shoes

Shoes are a girl's best friend too

Shoes reflect your personality. One can easily make out if you love comfort over fashion, or love casual over formal. The more pairs you have, the less it may seem; especially if you are a woman! Choose your shoes with caution as they can be overwhelming as well as uncomfortable if you are wearing a wrong pair. Let me list the top ten essential shoes for every woman. Although it may not be necessary for you to purchase all of them in this order; but you can certainly get a lot of insight from this list. This is but an indication about the basic shoes that you might require to complement your wardrobe.

Top ten

Low-heeled comfortable black pumps/peep toes

A low-heeled, comfortable black pump or a peep toe is essential to every woman's shoe collection for all those times when a strappy sandal or overly-glamorous shoe is inappropriate or too dressy. Like an early dinner, an impromptu business meeting, or even a funeral are the times when you will need them the most.

Black pumps

Neutral pumps or peep toes

Black pumps look versatile, but they do not go with every dress. So add a neutral pump or a peep toe to your collection for that classic look; one that goes with all the other shades of your western wear and smart strappy peep toes for Indian wear.

Neutral pumps

Semi-casual shoes

This will go with your jeans on the semi-casual office wear day. This will also be a comfortable pair with tights or jeans for occasions where sneakers will look absurd and tacky. Jeans with sneakers are for the teens and tiny-tots, not for women.

Semi-casual shoes

High-heeled dressy shoes

Nothing too strappy, nothing too trendy – but the basic black, dressy high heel is definitely an essential in any wardrobe. Occasions such as presentations, corporate luncheons or dinners, press conferences are the places to wear these classic pair. You can exhibit poise and style with such a pair. Make sure that you are comfortable walking in them.

High-heeled shoes

Killer evening shoes

Girly night outs, parties, or occasions where you need to put your glamorous foot forward. Such occasions are ideal to wear these shoes. Metallic or shoes with diamante or metallic studs are the best bets. Shoes with floral pieces, satin finish too look great. Shoes like these are ideal with pastels, silver, greys, and whites, and will also look fab with black dresses.

Killer evening shoes

Walking shoes

Walking or gym shoes

Gym shoes, walking shoes or exercise shoes are a really important pair in a woman's wardrobe. The choice is yours, whether it's a white sporty sneaker, or an edgy, black high top, every wardrobe needs a pair of comfortable sneakers. A good quality pair will avoid any injuries to your joints and muscles and, moreover will give comfort while you involve yourself in any strenuous activity.

Chic casual heels or ankle boots

Going for shopping or casual meeting, these pairs will instantly perk up your look when you pair it up with jeans. This will add some height as well as attitude to your look. Look for casual booties or shoes with a bit of a heel for times when you want to be chic, even in your pair of jeans.

Chic casual heels and ankle boots

Tall boots

Whether it's a high-heeled fashion boot or a warm and comfy casual style; a colder weather would require boots (We're not talking about the sheep skin bulky kinds; they only look good on Eskimos). Depending on the height of the boots you choose, everything from skirts to jeans can look fantastic with them. Every woman's wardrobe should have at least one pair in brown or black boots. I like boots with a low heel that can go casual or dressy.

Tall boots

Strappy sandals to go with your dresses

There are occasions when you like to go all girly and dressy. Strappy sandals or gladiators are the best bet for those times. Wear them with skirts, shirt dresses, t-dresses, but avoid them with capris and shorts. They are a comfortable alternative to sneakers or ballerinas which give enough room for your feet to breathe. These help to highlight your feminine side and can also make your overall look very appealing.

Strappy sandals

Comfortable at-home-slippers

Whatever shoes you wear during the day, your feet will appreciate being pampered at night when you slip on comfortable rubber or plastic slippers. Heels, tight-fitted closed shoes, and various other textures, play havoc with your feet the entire day. At home, try to give your feet some breathing space. Wear comfortable slip-ons at home to relax your feet muscles and help them rejuvenate. Many have started using 'Spa' like slippers for ultimate comfort around their home. Do not wear these to the supermarket or for walks in the park. Keep them only for home wear.

Slippers

Everyday shoes

Everyday shoes

A walk down the lane or meeting your next-door neighbour for a quick discussion and this pair is bound to grab eyes. This versatile pair goes well with skirts, jeans, and trousers. Comfort, fit, and style are key to choosing the right shoes for your everyday wear. This pair is ideal with those quick sprints to the neighbourhood grocery store, ATMs, and laundry.

Shoes should be bought keeping in mind your ankles and calves. If you wear a wrong pair of shoes, thick ankles, or calves might look like tree trunks and thin legs can look all the more tiny.

A few pointers to choose the right pair

Thick ankles

If you have thick ankles you should not wear flat shoes with pointed toes. That will make your legs look bulkier. High ankle shoes would make your ankle look strangulated and a very low thin heel will look a mismatch to your heavy ankle. Delicate heels highlight a thick ankle. Sling back shoes with small and thin heels, peep toe shoe with small and thin heel would look absurd on thick ankles.

A more chunkier and visible shoe would balance out the heavy structure. A simple thong wedge heel slippers or flat loafers will slim down the ankle as well as add length to your legs. Court pumps should have straight heels to elongate your legs else they may make your legs appear bulkier. Chunkier mid length or high heels would make your ankle appear slim.

Thin ankles

Thin ankles should avoid chunkier heels as they will appear all the more small. Even a ballet pump with extensive details like florals will overpower the small ankle. You do not wish to make your ankles look like a twig. If you want to wear open back slip-ons, make sure that they are thong sandals to make your legs appear in proportion. You can wear pointed toe and fine heels without any problem. Keep the design simple and delicate for your shoes. Elegant heels will make your legs appear delicate but not too thin.

Boot etiquette

Never tuck your trousers into ankle boots. Wear tights or skinny jeans instead. Pull on boots are the answer if you have bulky calves.

Make sure that the length of the boots does not end on the heaviest part of the calves.

Take a longer or a shorter length boot surrounding the calf area.

Wearing shoes is a part of dressing up. Make your shoes add newer dimensions to your personality, making you appear attractive and suave. Go for comfort, fit, and quality. Cheap ones do not last; neither do they make a lasting impression on anyone. So buy good quality shoes. Be practical while choosing a pair. Keep them clean and well maintained. Dirty and broken shoes are a big turn off.

Use your head while choosing your heels, I mean shoes.

Epilogue

So what are you waiting for? You just finished reading the book, now it's time to implement these changes. Gradually the change will show its effect and you will look fabulous in your new avatar.

It is your right to look and feel good. So go for it.

Bibliography

Sl No.	Image name	Copyright	Pg No.
1.	What do I buy? What will look good on me?	©Redbaron | Dreamstime.com	11
2.	Measurement	©Goran Kuzmanovski | Dreamstime.com	19
3.	Western wear	© Runjhun Gupta Dance addiction	30
4.	Indian Wear	©author- featuring Sharmistha Gupta	31
5.	Make-up	©Andi Berger | Dreamstime.com	32
6.	Clothing donations	©Carolyn Franks | Dreamstime.com	33
7.	Customised tailoring (colourful spools of thread)	©Julia Pivovarova | Dreamstime.com	34
10.	Customised tailoring (Sew essential)	© Tanya Brila | Dreamstime.com	34
11.	My style book	©Yuri Arcurs | Dreamstime.com	44
12.	Formal dress	©Duard Van Der Westhuizen | Dreamstime.com	49
13.	Business casual dress	©Editorial | Dreamstime.com	50
14.	Funeral and memorial service wear	©Tatiana Morozova | Dreamstime.com	51
15.	Holiday dressing	©Darren Green | Dreamstime.com	53
16.	Cocktail dress	©Make -up and Hair - Art of make up by Manishi jain, Model - Eisha Chopra, photographer - Anushka Nadia Menon	54
17.	Sweat shirts	© Nikola Hristovski | Dreamstime.com	61
18.	Nude hose with sandals	© Ragne Kabanova | Dreamstime.com	64
19.	Headgear	© Editorial | Dreamstime.com	66
20.	Mirrors and feathers	© Olga Vasilkova | Dreamstime.com	66
21.	Jewellery	©Olga Ekaterincheva | Dreamstime.com	67
22.	Chunky army boots	© Radu Razvan Gheorghe | Dreamstime.com	68
23.	Pink tummy shaper	©Ivan Polushkin | Dreamstime.com	72
24.	Choose right hair colour	©Andrew Taylor | Dreamstime.com	90

25.	Hair care	©Andrew Taylor | Dreamstime.com	97
26.	Hair fall and oil	©Lyudmyla Raynard | Dreamstime.com	98
27.	Hair colour chart	©Pixelife/ Dreamstime.com	100
28.	Exercise	©Sergei Popov | Dreamstime.com	102
29.	Hair spa	©Lkyam / Dreamstime.com	103
30.	Do not overdo heat treatment	©Dash/ Dreamstime.com	104
31.	Makeup kit	©Agnieszka Pastuszak - Maksim | Dreamstime.com	108
32.	Eye shapes	©Kurhan/ Dreamstime.com	116
33.	Nose look slimmer	©Nobeastsofierce | Dreamstime.com	117
34.	Fuller lips	©Daniel Wiedemann | Dreamstime.com	118
35.	Air Brush gun	©Sparmax, The Art of Makeup	120
36.	Glamorous red carpet look	©Valuavital..../ Dreamstime.com	121
37.	Femme Fatale look	©Seprimoris / Dreamstime.com	122
38.	Rock chic look	©Seprimoris / Dreamstime.com	122
39.	Natural look	©Kapu / Dreamstime.com	123
40.	Gothic look	©Smartfoto / Dreamstime.com	123
41.	Applying primer	© Adam Borkowski | Dreamstime.com	125
42.	Applying concealer	©Artem Mazunov | Dreamstime.com	127
43.	Applying eyeliner	©Vatikaki / Dreamstime.com	127
44.	Applying Kajal	©Sswartz / Dreamstime.com	128
45.	Applying eye shadow	©Daura Alytiene | Dreamstime.com	128
46.	Applying Mascara	©Konstantin Tavrov | Dreamstime.com	129
47.	Overplucked eyebrow	©Vladimir Mucibabic | Dreamstime.com	129
48.	Blush	©Eduardo Calazans | Dreamstime.com	130
49.	Lip liner	©Fritz Langmann | Dreamstime.com	130
50.	Don't apply lipstick on chapped lips	©Kitsen | Dreamstime.com	131
51.	Lip gloss	©Aleksey Telnov | Dreamstime.com	131
52.	Bronzer	©Ivosevicv / Dreamstime.com	131
53.	Metallic and glitter makeup	©Seprimoris / Dreamstime.com	132

54.	Pinks and reds	©Frenk And Danielle Kaufmann | Dreamstime.com	132
55.	Blues and greens	©Kaleenakatt | Dreamstime.com	133
56.	Loose powder	©Olga Vasilkova | Dreamstime.com	133
57.	Overload of makeup	©Olga Vasilkova | Dreamstime.com	133
58.	Highlighter	©Showface / Dreamstime.com	134
59.	Day time makeup	©Ruediger Baun | Dreamstime.com	134
60.	Bleaching facial hair	©Eastwest Imaging | Dreamstime.com	135
61.	Nail polish	©Serghei Starus | Dreamstime.com	136
62.	Wax strips	©Hamsterman | Dreamstime.com	137
63.	Too many scrubs and facials	©Adam Borkowski | Dreamstime.com	138
64.	Make up brushes and sponge	©Olga Vasilkova | Dreamstime.com	138
65.	Forgetting to tone	©Marko Plevnjak | Dreamstime.com	139
66.	Delicate skin around the eyes	©Francois Etienne Du Plessis | Dreamstime.com	143
67.	Chemical peels	©Anna Karwowska | Dreamstime.com	144
68.	Botox and Galvanic treatment	©Gabriel Blaj | Dreamstime.com	146
69.	Thermage skin firming treatment	©Serghei Starus | Dreamstime.com	147
70.	Dark chocolate facial	©Marek Kosmal | Dreamstime.com	149
71.	Wine facial	©Marek Pietrzak | Dreamstime.com	151
72.	Caviar	©Dmitry Maslov | Dreamstime.com	151
73.	Handbags	© Duron123 / Dreamstime.com	154
74.	Belts	©Vevesoran | Dreamstime.com	157
75.	Fashion jewellery	©Photomorgana | Dreamstime.com	158
76.	Black pumps	©Ewa Walicka / Dreamstime.com	163
77.	Semi casual shoes	©Dmitry Ternovoy | Dreamstime.com	164
78.	Tall boots	©Aleksandr Lobanov | Dreamstime.com	164
79.	Slippers	©Radu Razvan Gheorghe | Dreamstime.com	167